EVERYTHING
YOU EVER WANTED TO KNOW ABOUT
CLASSICAL
MUSIC

CLASSIC *f*M HANDY GUIDES

EVERYTHING
YOU EVER WANTED TO KNOW ABOUT
CLASSICAL
MUSIC

DARREN HENLEY

First published 2015 by
Elliott and Thompson Limited
27 John Street
London WC1N 2BX
www.eandtbooks.com

ISBN: 978-1-78396-157-3

Formerly published in 2012 as *Everything You Ever Wanted to
Know About Classical Music But Were Too Afraid to Ask*

9 8 7 6 5 4 3 2 1

A catalogue record for this book is available from the
British Library.

Typesetting: Marie Doherty
Printed in the UK by TJ International Ltd

For Izzy, who turned out to be rather good at this music thing.

Contents

Introduction   ix

Preface   xiii

Before We Get Started   xix

1   Early Music   1

2   The Baroque Period   21

3   The Classical Period   51

4   The Early Romantics   79

5   The Nationalist Romantics   103

6   The Late Romantics   137

7   The 20th Century   169

8   The 21st Century   209

Conclusion   245

Where To Find Out More   249

Acknowledgements   255

About the Author 257

Index 261

Introduction

At Classic FM, we spend a lot of our time dreaming up wonderful ways of making sure that as many people as possible across the UK have the opportunity to listen to classical music. As the nation's biggest classical music radio station, we feel that we have a responsibility to share the world's greatest music as widely as we can.

Over the years, we have written a variety of classical music books in all sorts of shapes and sizes. But we have never pulled together a series of books quite like this.

This set of books covers a whole range of aspects of classical music. They are all written in Classic FM's friendly, accessible style and you can rest assured that they are packed full of facts about classical music. Read separately, each book gives you a handy snapshot of a particular subject area. Added together, the series combines to offer a more detailed insight into the full story of classical music. Along the way, we shall be paying particular attention to some of the key composers whose music we play most often on the radio station, as well as examining many of classical music's sub genres.

This particular book is rather longer than those that make up the rest of the series, providing you with a pocket-sized overview of classical music. However, it is still relatively small in size, so it is not going to be encyclopedic in its level of detail; there are other books out there that do that much better than we could ever hope to. We have included a list of them in the chapter entitled 'Where To Find Out More' towards the end of this book.

Instead, our series of *Classic FM Handy Guides* is intended to form an enjoyable introduction that will be particularly useful to listeners who are beginning their voyage of discovery through the rich and exciting world of classical music. Drawing on the research and previous writing we have undertaken for many of our other Classic FM books, such as *The A–Z of Classic FM Music*, *The Classic FM Friendly Guide to Music* and *Everything You Ever*

Wanted to Know About Classical Music . . . But Were Too Afraid to Ask, this particular title concentrates on information rather than theory because we want to make it attractive and inviting to readers who are not necessarily familiar with the more complex aspects of musicology.

For more information on this series, take a look at our website: www.ClassicFM.com/handyguides.

Preface

This book is a revised edition of Classic FM's popular *Everything You Ever Wanted to Know About Classical Music . . . But Were Too Afraid to Ask*, originally published in 2012. This new edition has been both condensed to focus on the history of classical music and updated to include a wider range of composers.

We are often asked the question 'What exactly is classical music?' It is probably something we ought to tackle before getting going on our journey through the genre's history.

The strictest definition of classical music is everything that was written in the Classical period (between 1750 and 1830), but today we understand classical music to be much more than music composed in just those eighty years.

Calling a piece of music 'classical' is sometimes done as a means of generically distinguishing it from 'popular' music. One of the major tests of whether a tune is or isn't classical music has traditionally been whether it has a sense of 'permanence' about it, in that it is still being performed many years after its composition. This argument begins to fall down as the heritage of pop music becomes ever longer, with hits from the 1950s still being played on the radio today, well over half a century after their original release. It is also hard for us to tell whether a newly written piece of classical music will indeed attain a level of 'permanence' in the future.

The *Concise Oxford Dictionary of Music* offers the following as one of its definitions of classical music: 'Music of an orderly nature, with qualities of clarity and balance, and emphasising formal beauty rather than emotional expression (which is not to say that emotion is lacking)'.

It is true to say that much of classical music follows specific rules of style and form, the development of which we will discuss in the chapters that follow. However, this definition still does not quite do the job.

One of the most striking differences between classical and pop music is the different way the two genres place emphasis on the relative importance of the composer and the performer. In pop music the performer is all, but in classical music the composer is the star of the show. It is his or her name that tends to come first in the credits and it is he or she who is remembered by history. Take Mozart's *Clarinet Concerto* as an example. Not many people remember Anton Stadler, the clarinettist for whom it was written, but everyone knows Mozart's name. Conversely, if you ask most music fans whom they would associate with that hardy perennial 'White Christmas', they would reply 'Bing Crosby', rather than the song's composer, Irving Berlin.

At Classic FM, we have long believed that film scores sit firmly inside the world of classical music. The first dedicated soundtrack was composed by Camille Saint-Saëns for the 1908 film *L'Assassinat du duc de Guise*. Since then, Aaron Copland, Ralph Vaughan Williams, William Walton, Sergei Prokofiev and Dmitri Shostakovich have all written music for the cinema. If we go back to the time of Beethoven, we find him composing incidental music for the theatre of the day. Had cinema been invented in his lifetime, he would undoubtedly have written this genre of music too.

Today, film soundtracks are among the most popular symphonic works being composed, with pieces by the likes of John Williams, Hans Zimmer, Howard Shore and James Horner providing an excellent gateway into wider listening to classical music.

Throughout classical music's history, composers have always written music for those who pay, whether their patrons were rich noblemen or rich film studios. In the past few years, the more commercial end of classical music has included scores especially written for video games. We will discuss this later in the book, but make no mistake, companies such as EA Games are now among the biggest commissioners of contemporary classical composers and many of our greatest symphony orchestras are earning significant income from recording long-form symphonic works specifically for inclusion as soundtracks on video games. It would be wrong to ignore this pivotal development in the story of classical music, simply because it is commercial in nature and relatively new as a concept.

Whatever the definition of classical music to which you personally subscribe, we think that the great jazz trumpeter Louis Armstrong had things just about right when he said, 'There's only two ways to sum up music: either it's good or it's bad. If it's good you don't mess about it – you just enjoy it.'

We hope you will enjoy uncovering the rich tapestry of sounds, emotions and stories that go together to make up classical music. It is the greatest music ever written. We also hope that you will enjoy the Classic FM radio programme that accompanies this book, presented by the acclaimed singer and broadcaster Catherine Bott every Sunday evening at nine o'clock. At more than 150 episodes, *Everything You Ever Wanted to Know About Classical Music* is one of the biggest non-fiction series in the history of British radio.

Before We Get Started

In common with the other books in the *Classic FM Handy Guides* series, we have tried to make this book as easy to use as possible.

The chapters that follow neatly divide up classical music into a series of eras. Of course, classical music is all about the listening, rather than just being about the reading, so we have put together a handy playlist at the end of each chapter.

You will find these same playlists on our website at www.ClassicFM.com/handyguides. Here, you will be able to find ways of purchasing the relevant tracks, so that you can listen along while you read. These lists are by no means exhaustive, but we hope they will offer an introduction to each of the featured composer's best-known or most significant works. As always with this sort of recommendation, there is a good deal of subjectivity involved, so we have tended to opt, in most cases, for the works that are most often featured on air on Classic FM.

One final word about the style that we use in all of the books in this series:

- Titles of all musical works are set in italics;
- Songs and arias appear in italics within quotation marks;
- Nicknames for a particular work also appear in italics with quotation marks, usually after the work's formal title.

Happy listening!

one

Early Music

In the Beginning

Music has been around for a long time. Historians have no doubt about that, although there are differing opinions about exactly when and where the idea of making musical instruments to play tunes first took hold. Fragments of primitive instruments, crafted more than ten centuries ago, have been found by archaeologists in places as far apart as Germany, Spain, Egypt and China.

Human beings are inherently musical. We can make all sorts of sounds with just our bodies, and the earliest musicians probably had no need for instrumental add-ons at all. Singing, clapping and even foot-tapping are all forms of music. In fact, they are used today as a means of teaching very young children about the rudiments of making music.

When we talk about 'Early Music' in the classical music world, it's in fact an umbrella term for two, sometimes three, periods in music prior to the Classical period. Usually, it means the combined music of both the Medieval and Renaissance periods, although some definitions take in Baroque as being early, too. We don't think that is the case and treat the Baroque period as being a completely separate entity.

The Medieval and Renaissance periods together cover just about all music-making up until 1600, with the Medieval era ending at 1400. Although there was undoubtedly music-making before AD 500, this is the rough date from which many musical histories start. The Renaissance sub-period of Early Music covers the two centuries between 1400 and 1600.

Aside from this date-based definition, Early Music is sometimes used today as a term for music that has been rediscovered in our time, and for which authentic forms of performance are pursued. This is sometimes known as the 'Early Music Movement'.

What Else Was Going On in the World?

Well, in the year 985 or 986, the Viking Bjarni Herjolfsson was blown off course and sighted the coast of America. The continent was not discovered officially by a European for just over 500 years, when Christopher Columbus landed in the West Indies in 1492.

The dawning of the second millennium saw England under attack from the Danes. In 1012, the invading forces rampaged through Canterbury, although they were bought off with 48,000 pounds of silver.

King Canute ruled England from 1016 to 1035 and King Harold was briefly on the throne in 1066 until William the Conqueror took over the crown following the Battle of Hastings. Scotland's kings included Macbeth from 1040 to 1057.

In fact, what we consider now to be Early Music was composed right through the time that England was reigned over by members of the House of Plantagenet (1154–1399), the House of Lancaster (1399–1461), the House of York (1461–1485) and the House of Tudor, ending with the reign of Elizabeth I between 1558 and 1603. In Scotland,

James VI was on the throne from 1567, becoming James I of England following Elizabeth I's death in 1603.

This period encompasses the Crusades, the signing of the Magna Carta, the devastating scourge of the Black Death across Europe and the Hundred Years War between Britain and France, from 1337 to 1453.

So, the world was a busy place, with warfare at the top of many people's agendas as one tribe or nation plotted to take over another, only to find their efforts reversed a few years later. However, as you will see, there were huge developments in music, many of which were brought about by the Catholic Church.

Ambrose and Gregory

Although the title above sounds like a 1970s television sitcom, Ambrose was in fact Bishop of Milan between 374 and 397; and Gregory I was Pope between 590 and 604. Among the latter's many claims to fame was his decision to send Augustine to England to convert the locals to Christianity.

Between 500 and 1400, the principal surviving

music is plainsong. It had been handed down for centuries already by the year 500. Bishop Ambrose and Pope Gregory are generally credited with making great strides in the evolution of plainsong, which was the unaccompanied singing that took place as part of church services, most often performed by monks.

Ambrose was an important figure in the development of antiphonal singing, where two parts of a choir sing alternately with the second section answering the first. Gregory's contribution is, however, more often remembered by musical historians, and he is given the credit for a more general overhaul of this area of music a couple of hundred years later. He gave his name to the result, and Gregorian Chant was born. He was responsible for formalising chant through his Schola Cantorum, which was not just a papal choir but a whole system of handing down choir music from generation to generation. He also produced publications such as *The Antiphonar*, a compendium of chants.

Hitting the Right Note

People had been trying to write down music for a while by the start of the second millennium, but there was no truly uniform method for making a record of exactly who had to sing what and when, and for how long.

We know that instrumental music was also being made in the centuries before the end of the first millennium, but there is no accurate record of what sort of tunes were being composed, so we can only imagine how they might have sounded.

As ancient and far removed as this period may seem to us now, it was a time of amazing and exciting developments. In around 1025, a monk called **Guido d'Arezzo** (c. 955–c. 1050) published his theories on musical notation. He had developed a system that meant chants could be read and then sung by anyone who had learned to decipher the code that he had created. Today, we call this deciphering 'reading music'.

For this reason, we are able to understand and give authentic performances of music written 1,000 years ago. It means that the heritage of classical music has been preserved in a way that other musical genres from around the world simply have not been. We have a lot to thank Guido d'Arezzo for.

The Really Early Composers

The first composer in this era is a woman. She is, in fact, one of very few female composers in this book. Equal opportunity does not seem to have played a great part in the development of much of classical music, although the announcement of Judith Weir as the first female Master of the Queen's Music in 2014 was perhaps the start of a long-needed rebalancing of the genders in the genre.

Hildegard of Bingen (1098–1179) was born into a noble family, and was sent away to a monastery at the age of just eight. By the time she was thirty-eight, she had become the leader of the nuns who were based at the monastery and, around twelve years later, she founded her own nunnery near the town of Bingen.

Hildegard was no ordinary nun. Apart from having a gift for writing poetry and music, she became an influential diplomat, corresponding regularly with religious and secular leaders. As a thinker, she made her name in areas such as science and medicine.

Hildegard became famed as a mystic and, between 1141 and 1170, she had no fewer than twenty-six visions. She wrote down their details and set them to music.

People travelled from far and wide to consult Hildegard, and when she died at the age of eighty-one (a remarkable achievement in itself at the time), the Catholic Church considered making her a saint, although it was not until 2012 that she was finally canonised by Pope Benedict XVI.

This period of Early Music also included the delightful round, '*Sumer is icumen in*', often attributed to the Norfolk-born **John of Fornsete** (d. 1238/9). Worthy of mention, too, is **Franco of Cologne** (active in the 1250s), a German composer who standardised the measure of notes by codifying the length and appearance of minims, breves, crotchets, and so on.

After 1300, the *ars antiqua* was replaced by the *ars nova*, when plainchant gave way to polyphony – separate tunes for people with voices singing at different pitches (sopranos, tenors, basses, etc.), which all combine together harmoniously.

Some composers lived for the moment and others spent their time worrying about their legacy. One of the principal driving forces in the development of musical polyphony, **Guillaume de Machaut** (c. 1300–1377), was firmly in the latter camp, although he was not without talent: he counted Geoffrey Chaucer among his fans. In particular, Machaut is remembered for developing new ways of using rhythm.

Machaut became a canon in Reims when he was about forty, and he seems to have spent much of the rest of his life bossing around the monks who were instructed to reproduce copies of his complete works. His desire for musical immortality was not in vain and he is one of the best-known composers of the period, simply because so much of his music still survives.

Although he was a priest, this doesn't seem to have stopped Machaut writing extensively on the subject of unfulfilled passion, and many of his songs were not religious at all. Instead, he adopted the style of the troubadours, wandering poets and musicians who performed their work in the homes of the French nobility.

However, it's for his four-part Mass that Machaut is most respected. He was among the first composers to write four separate tunes for people with different voices, which combined together harmoniously, and this was a big step forward in the history of classical music. This new style of singing was known as polyphony.

The Renaissance Men

As you will discover as our story unfolds, there are periods in the history of classical music where similar developments occurred simultaneously in different countries. One of the big times of change in classical music was what we now call the Renaissance Period, from around 1400 to 1600, which saw a rapid rebirth of styles and ideas about how music should be composed. Literally translated from the French, renaissance means 'rebirth'.

The British tend to think of **John Dunstable** (c. 1390–1453) as heading up their group (or 'school') of Renaissance composers, while in France, it was the Belgian **Guillaume Dufay** (c. 1397–1474) who was carrying the torch for the rebirth. The Renaissance was not just going on in the world of music; the new discoveries also spanned science, exploration and the visual arts.

John Dunstable was one of English music's greatest exports and, rather like The Beatles in the 1960s, he was very much the face of English music abroad in the mid-1400s. Composers around Europe were impressed by his style of writing and incorporated many of his new ideas into their own compositions. All of this popularity led to Dunstable becoming something of a property magnate back home, with a string of houses to his name across the south of England.

Almost all of the music Dunstable wrote was for use in church, and he managed to create a particularly rich sound. Guillaume Dufay was one of the Continental composers who was influenced by Dunstable's music.

Dufay was the illegitimate son of a priest and began his musical career as a boy chorister at Cambrai Cathedral. He moved on to Bologna in Italy and worked for the Pope in Rome and Florence. In the 1450s, Dufay composed a Mass based on a folk song called *'L'Homme armé'*, which translates as *'The Armed Man'*. He was one of a long line of composers in musical history to use this title for a Mass – the most recent of whom is the Welshman Karl Jenkins, whose *The Armed Man: A Mass for Peace* was premiered in 2000.

Dufay wrote every sort of music that had been invented at the time, including a wider variety of religious music and a range of secular songs. Word has it that he was also the first composer to write a Requiem Mass, but this is hard to prove definitively because the manuscript has been lost.

It's easy to become confused about our next composer, **John Taverner** (c. 1490–1545). Don't mistake him for John Tavener (without the extra 'r'), who was a renowned choral composer of the late twentieth and early twenty-first centuries. We will come to him much later, in Chapter 8.

John Taverner was one of the big stars of English music in this period. As well as being a composer, he was a friend of Thomas Cromwell, one of the main forces behind the dissolution of the monasteries. It is possible that Taverner was a supporter of these reforms; he is on record as saying that he was embarrassed to have penned 'popish ditties' early on in his career as a composer. This idea is explored in a 1970 opera called *Taverner*, which was written by Sir Peter Maxwell Davies. Again, more on him much later on in this book (see Chapter 8).

Thomas Tallis (c. 1505–1585) was another mighty force in English music. He was composing throughout the reigns of Henry VIII, who broke away from Rome and created the Church of England; Edward VI; Mary I, who was Catholic; and Elizabeth I, who was Protestant. Considering that Tallis managed to write music for the Church during all four of these reigns, he must have been as good at bending his style to suit the prevailing wind as he was at composing the music in the first place. Tallis is known for his church music in general, such as his *Mass for Four Voices* and his *Lamentations*; the staggeringly beautiful *'Spem in alium'* is possibly his most breathtaking work, an amazingly skilful combination of forty separate vocal parts.

Tallis's exact provenance has been lost in the mists of time, but he was probably brought up near Canterbury, working first as an organist at Dover Priory. He then moved to Waltham Abbey in Essex in the same role, before becoming a lay clerk at Canterbury Cathedral.

From 1543 until his death more than four decades later, Tallis operated a job share with his pupil **William Byrd** (c. 1540–1623) as the composer and organist to the Chapel Royal. Byrd was known as 'the father of British music'. The fact that he survived to write anything at all is surprising, considering that he was known to be a Catholic supporter at a time when this was punishable by death. He became organist and choirmaster at Lincoln Cathedral in 1563, where he stayed until 1572 when he moved to London to take up the job share with Thomas Tallis.

Whereas Tallis wrote only a few pieces that were not for the Church, Byrd left behind some excellent examples of keyboard music and of madrigals (unaccompanied songs for a group of voices).

Byrd and Tallis lived out their lives in relative financial comfort because of the beneficence of Elizabeth I. She granted them jointly a patent that allowed them a complete monopoly on printing music and music paper in England for twenty-one years from 1575. Their first publication was called *Cantiones Sacrae*, which translates as 'Sacred Songs'. It was made up of a total of thirty-four different songs – seventeen by each composer.

This new means of distributing music meant that, for the first time, choirs could sing music from printed sheets, making it far easier for musical works to become established right across the country.

Back to Italy now, and it is important to remember that innovation in sacred music was not necessarily welcomed with open arms by the Catholic Church. Some of the changes were even the subject of papal decrees. With the rise of Protestantism, any modification of the status quo tended to be regarded as an all-out attack on the foundations of the Church itself. Some senior members of the Church even advocated changing things back to the style written by composers of the likes of Hildegard of Bingen, because they believed that the fancy new way of writing music meant that the sacred texts no longer had the same powerful meaning.

Giovanni Pierluigi da Palestrina (c. 1525–1594) took his name from the pleasant hillside town near Rome where he was born. Chiefly a choral composer, Palestrina followed his employer, the Bishop of Palestrina, to Rome when the Bishop became Pope Julius III.

When he was asked to compose a Mass that would definitively prove one way or another whether polyphony really was the way forward for church music, rather than the plainsong of old.

Palestrina produced a Mass that was so beautiful that the critics gave up and the polyphonic brigade was victorious. He dedicated this new piece, which was composed around 1561, to Pope Marcellus.

The Pope reigned for only fifty-five days and never actually heard the music that was written especially for him.

Palestrina had some particularly unhappy periods during his life. In the 1570s, his family was torn
apart by the plague, which was sweeping through
Europe with devastating consequences. His wife,
brother and two of his sons all succumbed to the
terrible disease.

We now stay in Italy for the rest of this period
of classical music. As you will see as our story continues, there were strong English, French, Austrian,
German, Russian and Eastern European influences
on classical music at various times in its history.
Italy could argue the case for being the most influential country of all – and nowhere has that Italian
influence been more keenly felt than in the world
of opera.

Opera was a really major development in classical music. In its most basic form, opera marks the
coming together of words and music in an equal
partnership.

The man to whom history has given credit for
writing the world's first opera is one **Jacopo Peri**
(1561–1633) whose first operatic work was *Dafne*.
The composer himself was something of a performer and he took the role of Apollo in the first
production in 1598. Although we know the opera

performance took place, the music has now been lost. However, Peri's second opera, *Euridice*, does still exist and is occasionally performed today.

Although he has no right to claim the title at all, many people consider **Claudio Monteverdi's** (1567–1643) *La Favola d'Orfeo* to be the first true opera. It's based on the same story as *Euridice*. Orpheus (Orfeo) and Euridice are husband and wife in the mythological tale. The story goes that Orpheus was so distraught at Euridice's death that he visited Hades, the land of the dead, to try to get her back. He ultimately fails in his quest. It was a story to which other composers returned time and time again during later periods of classical music.

Monteverdi is also known today for his sacred music, and in particular for his *Vespers for the Blessed Virgin*, dedicated to Pope Paul V. This is a strikingly beautiful piece of music, which was written shortly after both Monteverdi's wife and his only child had died. It is quite likely that his own personal suffering is mirrored in the music.

The End of Early Music

The advent of opera marks the end of the longest period of music in this book. It began at the dawn of time, or around the year 1000, depending on your point of view, and ended at around the turn of the seventeenth century.

It is worth noting at this point that the beginning and end of each musical era cannot be pinpointed to an absolute moment in time. One set of composers did not simply stop writing, to be replaced by a new team waiting patiently on the subs' bench. Instead, new styles of music gradually replaced old styles – just as plainchant gave way to polyphony and Medieval composers were replaced by Renaissance composers, so they in turn faded away. You will be relieved to know that our story most certainly doesn't end there, though.

Handy Early Music Playlist

1 Hildegard of Bingen: *'A Feather on the Breath of God'*
2 Guillaume de Machaut: *Messe de Notre Dame*
3 John Dunstable: *Preco preheminencie*
4 John Taverner: *Mass: 'The Western Wynde'*
5 Thomas Tallis: *'Spem in alium'*
6 William Byrd: *'Ave verum corpus'*

7   Giovanni Pierluigi da Palestrina: *Missa Papae Marcelli*

8   Jacopo Peri: *Euridice*

9   Claudio Monteverdi: *Vespers for the Blessed Virgin*

two

The Baroque Period

Baroque 'n' Roll

Had this book been written by an American, the heading above would probably have been 'If it ain't baroque, don't fix it', because our cousins across the Atlantic pronounce the world 'Baroque' with a long 'o', so the second syllable rhymes with 'poke'. But back here in Britain, we pronounce it with a short 'o', to rhyme with 'clock'.

What Else Was Going On in the World?

Anyway, enough of the pronunciation guide. We are now in the period of classical music that runs from 1600 to 1750. This was a rather exciting time

in history, with plenty of storylines for action movies: Guy Fawkes attempted to blow up the Houses
of Parliament in the Gunpowder Plot; the Pilgrim
Fathers set sail on the *Mayflower* from Plymouth for
a new life in America; and Charles I was beheaded.
It was also a period of enormous scientific advance-
ment: Isaac Newton realised that the earth had a
gravitational pull, so the story goes, after being hit
on the head by an apple, and astronomers also
decided once and for all that the earth orbits the
sun, rather than vice versa.

Big Changes Afoot

Originally an architectural term, Baroque translates
literally from the French as 'bizarre', although the
Portuguese word *barocco*, meaning 'a rare, funny-
shaped pearl', is its true ancestor. In music, it
covers the period that spans, roughly, the 150 years
between 1600 and 1750.

Like its architectural counterpart, Baroque
music must have seemed somewhat bizarre to the
musical old guard in and around 1600. Its intrica-
cies, particularly those of its harmonies, became
more and more complex over the years. In Early
Music, harmony developed fairly slowly; its tunes

possessed an inner simplicity all of their own. In the Baroque period, the notion of harmonic change just took off, while melodies became positively hyperactive (just listen to a fast movement from any of Bach's *Brandenburg Concertos* to prove this point).

Another development was music's ability to picture something of real life, whether in terms of emotions and feelings or even musical representations of landscapes and weather patterns. This change was increasingly possible because music was moving out of its traditional church setting and into the homes and palaces of the nobility. Instrumental music, long fought against by the Church, was developing fast, with the coming of the sonata, the suite and the concerto grosso.

One other interesting shift that came in the Baroque period was the bass section acting more as a musical anchor than it had before. Previously, the bass part, whether vocal or instrumental, had been just one of the parts – as free as the other parts to wander where it pleased. In the Baroque era, the bass became the cornerstone of a musical work. It was less mobile than its counterparts and therefore more able to root the harmony.

From Church to Nobility

The Church was still an important force in deciding what music would be written, not least because it employed so many composers, in a variety of musical roles. However, as the story of the Baroque period unfurls, you will begin to notice a shift in power. Gradually, the Church becomes a less important force in the commissioning of new music, to be replaced by the nobility, who listened to music chiefly for recreational pleasure, rather than out of devotional duty, and who commissioned composers and employed musicians as a means of showing off their status within society.

We begin our journey through the Baroque composers with two men who are firmly in the sacred music camp.

Gregorio Allegri (1582–1652) was steeped in the traditions of the Catholic Church, becoming a choirboy at the age of nine and ending up as music director of the papal choir two years before his death.

He is best known today for his *Miserere*, which was performed every year during Holy Week from the time it was written until towards the end of the nineteenth century. The Vatican kept the lid on the exact details of what was being sung, and anyone who made an illegal copy of the music was threatened with severe punishment. The *Miserere* was probably even more stunning to listen to back in Allegri's time than it is today because the members of the highly skilled papal choir would add their own embellishments to the music – an example of seventeenth-century choral jamming, if you like. This piece of music also warrants a mention during the life of one Wolfgang Amadeus Mozart, on page 64 of this book.

The English composer **Orlando Gibbons** (1583–1625) was a member of the Chapel Royal. This choir still exists today and is an important part of the royal household's music-making. You will often see the choir performing at state occasions. The Chapel Royal was something of a hothouse for the best musical talent in England and, because it was the monarch's own choir, it was able to cherry-pick the very best musicians from all of the other choirs around the country. As well as Orlando Gibbons, Thomas Tallis, William Byrd and Henry Purcell were all important members of this august body.

Gibbons was a particularly talented organist,

and he also wrote keyboard works and pieces to
be performed by consorts (groups of musicians).
It is worth noting that Gibbons was the first major
composer to write exclusively for the Anglican
Church. He died tragically young while with the
royal household in Canterbury, where he is buried
in the cathedral.

Jean-Baptiste Lully (1632–1687) held a priv-
ileged position in the French court, working as the
personal composer to King Louis XIV. Although
Italian by birth, he is thought of as a great French
composer. A self-taught violinist, he worked as a
servant from the age of fourteen, before progress-
ing to become a dancer. In 1653, he began working
for Louis XIV as a composer of ballet music and
was quickly promoted. His job made him the most
important man in French music, and for more than
two decades he was able to exert enormous control
over the country's musical life.

During this time, Lully achieved a lot, particularly in developing the sound of the orchestra.
After his changes, orchestras looked and sounded
far closer to the ones we have today than they did
to those that had pre-dated him.

Lully was undoubtedly an innovator and a

visionary. Many of the instruments that he brought into the orchestra had only just been invented, so, although an orchestra made up of twenty-four violins plus flutes, oboes, bassoons, trumpets and timpani might seem normal to us, it was absolutely revolutionary in the 1600s.

Lully also bought the right to be the only man in France to be allowed to put on operas – he staged his first production on a converted tennis court. He was also extremely influential in the area of music publishing and became well known for writing ballets.

Lully's death was the stuff of legend. Rather than the conductor's baton that we know today, Lully used a long stick to beat time on the floor when he was conducting his orchestra. One day, he missed the floor and speared his own foot instead. Gangrene set in and he died two months later after refusing to have his foot amputated. His royal patronage did, however, ensure that he died an extremely rich man.

Although he lived at the same time as Lully, **Marc-Antoine Charpentier** (1643–1704) was never part of Louis XIV's court. His choral music has come back into fashion in recent years, but his best-known work is infamous for an altogether different reason. Next time you settle down in front of the television to watch the Eurovision Song Contest, listen to the opening theme music: it is the trumpet tune at the very start of Charpentier's *Te Deum*. You can rest assured that it will be just about the only piece of music that you hear all evening that doesn't deserve 'nul points'.

Italian **Arcangelo Corelli** (1653–1713) was born into a rich family and was lucky enough not to face the hand-to-mouth financial struggles that many other composers were forced to endure. Despite what some of the self-appointed grandees of the classical music world would have you believe, most composers tended to write music as a means of putting food on their tables, a roof over their heads and clothes on their backs, and not because of some sort of flight of artistic fancy.

Perhaps it was Corelli's relative wealth that made him less hungry to produce a copious amount of work, or perhaps because he didn't need to keep an eye on the money coming in he could spend more time refining his music, but he was by no means the most prolific composer of his time. He was, however, celebrated across Europe, and many of the greatest composers who followed him, such as Bach and Handel, were undoubtedly influenced by the music he wrote.

Corelli was an outstanding violin player, and he is the first of our featured composers to make a name purely from the composition of instrumental music. He also brought some new thinking to the way that orchestras performed, insisting that all the string players mirrored each other's playing style by moving their bows up and down in the same direction at the same time. This changed the sound made by the orchestra, allowing the musicians to give a more precise performance. It also made Corelli's orchestras visually far more aesthetically pleasing, and his concerts became popular because they were as easy on the eye as they were on the ear.

Corelli was also the master of the concerto grosso, a type of musical work where the orchestra is divided into two groups. One group of musicians tended to play first, with the other group then echoing the music. This created a sense of drama between the two groups of players and between the louder and quieter parts of the music.

At Classic FM, we have a term for those composers who are known for one great work that dwarfs all the rest of their output. We call them 'one-hit wonders'. The German **Johann Pachelbel** (1653–1706) is a prime example of the species, with his *Canon in D* a firm favourite in all sorts of environments, not least as an accompaniment to the walk down the aisle at many weddings.

Many composers wrote canons – but nobody else achieved quite the same fame for it. It's a simple idea in which a melody is played and then imitated by one or more other instruments or voices. You might unwittingly have performed a canon yourself as a child when you sang *'Frère Jacques'*, *'Three Blind Mice'*, or *'London's Burning'*. In these cases, when the following voices sing exactly the same tune as the initial voice, the canon is sometimes referred to as a 'round'.

Although the *Canon in D* is pretty much all he is remembered for now, Pachelbel was massive in the world of keyboard and chamber music in the late seventeenth century (any piece that is written for small groups of musicians to play counts as chamber music. We even have chamber orchestras, which are smaller than symphony orchestras and often feature up to around thirty players).

This book is filled to the brim with musical

prodigies and **Henry Purcell** (1659–1695) is the first of them. It is just as well that his talent was identified and nurtured while he was young, because he was just thirty-six years old when he died – although he achieved more than many compos ers who lived to be twice his age. Music historians say that his death was a real setback for the development of English music. It was not for another 200 years that England would produce another truly great composer, in the shape of Edward Elgar.

By the time Purcell was ten, he was one of the Children of the Chapel Royal (a choirboy). Just a decade later, he was given one of the most prestigious musical jobs of the moment when he was made organist of Westminster Abbey.

Purcell produced a large amount of music, considering his short life, and its range was wide – taking in organ solos, sacred anthems, secular songs, chamber music and music to be performed in the theatre. He wrote works for Charles II, James II and Queen Mary.

Purcell's only opera, *Dido and Aeneas*, tells the story of Dido, the Queen of Carthage. She is in love with Aeneas, who sails away to found Rome. She is devastated and sings the haunting aria '*When I Am*

Laid in Earth' – in our opinion the greatest thing
Purcell ever wrote.

Purcell went on to compose four large-scale
semi-operatic works in the early 1690s – *King Arthur*
is probably the best known of them – and the incidental music for numerous plays. On his untimely
death in 1695, he was buried in Westminster Abbey.
His tomb is still there, today, near the organ, alongside the inscription: 'Here lyes Henry Purcell Esq.,
who left this life and is gone to that blessed place
where only his harmony can be exceeded.'

Another English composer of the time,
Jeremiah Clarke (c. 1670–1707) suffered the
indignity of having his best-known work wrongly
attributed to Purcell for many years. Clarke also
worked as the organist at the Chapel Royal, before
moving on to Winchester College and St Paul's
Cathedral. He wrote *The Prince of Denmark's March*
in about 1700. Today, it is more popularly known as
the *Trumpet Voluntary.* It remains a popular choice
at wedding ceremonies, which seems unfortunate
because Clarke shot himself dead after the unhappy
ending of a love affair.

In another case of misattribution, our next composer is most famous for a piece of music that he

never actually completed (and quite possibly didn't actually write at all). The music that we regard as being the *Adagio in G minor* by **Tomaso Albinoni** (1671–1750) was (it's claimed) based on only a fragment of manuscript, rather than a fully realised work. This fragment was taken by an Italian professor, Remo Giazotto, who built it up into the piece we know and love today, based on his studies of the composer's other works. It would be fair to say that Giazotto took an informed guess as to how Albinoni intended the *Adagio* to turn out.

It's hard not to feel just a little sorry for Albinoni because there are plenty of other surviving pieces that he definitely did write, for which he could be remembered. The 300 or so works to his name include more than 50 operas and more than 50 concertos.

Antonio Vivaldi (1678–1741) was responsible for what many people reckon is the most recorded piece of classical music of all time: the *Four Seasons*. Every year, new versions are released, but for our money, it's hard to beat the 1989 version by Nigel Kennedy, originally on EMI Classics, and now available on the Warner Classics label.

It's all the more remarkable that this work has

achieved the success it has when you consider that Vivaldi's music was hardly played at all from his death in 1741 through until the middle of the twentieth century. This is all down to a rather strange decision by a nobleman called Count Giacomo Durazzo. He pulled together all of Vivaldi's original works and simply locked them up. In his last will and testament, Durazzo ordered his family to make sure that none of this music by Vivaldi should ever be performed or published. After many years, these ludicrous instructions were overturned and Vivaldi's music was once more heard. The public lapped up his catchy melodies, and a star was reborn, some 200 years after his death.

Vivaldi certainly rattled out the concertos, with more than 500 of them to his name. Unkind critics suggest that he actually wrote the same tune in a slightly different way 500 times, but we don't think that's entirely fair.

There is no doubt that Vivaldi was a bit of a character. He chose to follow in his father's footsteps and learned to play the violin. He played the instrument while undertaking his religious training, becoming known as 'The Red Priest' because of his bright red hair.

Vivaldi was excused having to say Mass because he claimed to suffer from asthma. The illness certainly didn't stop him from conducting or from travelling all over Europe. It also didn't prevent him from enjoying a close relationship with at least one of his travelling companions, a young soprano called Anna Girò, and quite possibly with her half-sister Paolina Trevisana as well. He was censured for unpriestly conduct, despite denying that his relationship with the two women was in any way improper.

Any illicit affairs certainly never got in the way of Vivaldi's composing, though. As well as the 500 concertos, he also wrote more than 50 operas, well over 80 sonatas and more than 120 other sacred and secular vocal pieces.

Alongside his work as a composer, he was head of the violins at La Pietà orphans institute, which had an impressive orchestra and chorus. He remained there, on and off, in various posts until he was thirty-eight. During this time he wrote many great instrumental works, including his now famous concertos and sonatas. Between the ages of thirty-eight and fifty, he worked variously out of Mantua and Rome, concentrating on opera, although he still composed 'by post' for La Pietà. He then ventured further afield – to Vienna and Prague – before returning to La Pietà as Maestro di Capella.

Late in life, he moved to Vienna in search of more opera commissions, only to be thwarted by the death of the Emperor Charles VI and the ensuing customary closure of all the opera houses during the official period of court mourning. He died, aged sixty-three, in relative poverty and was interred in the burial ground of the public hospital.

Giuseppe Tartini (1692–1770) was another Baroque composer who was torn between religious devotion and more earthly physical delights. Born in what was then part of northern Italy but is now Slovenia, Tartini intended to become a monk, but he had to rethink this after eloping with the bishop's daughter while studying at Padua University. Having married, the couple evaded the bishop's arrest warrant for three years, before Tartini was forced to leave town and his wife was sent to a convent. The composer took the opportunity to hole himself up in a monastery and perfect his amazing violin technique, returning to Padua, now pardoned, and staying there as head of the Cappella del Santo for the rest of his life. His compositions naturally reflect his supremacy as a violinist.

Although many of the great Baroque composers were without question prolific in their output, they are all mere minnows in terms of productivity when compared to our next composer. In the race to write the largest number of pieces, **Georg Philipp Telemann** (1681–1767) is not only miles ahead of the rest of the Baroque pack, he storms in front of every other composer featured so far – or in the pages still to come – with around 3,700 different works to his name. He wrote masses of music for more or less every instrumental or vocal combination.

He originally studied law at Leipzig University, following his parents' wishes, but soon switched to music, winning church posts in Leipzig, Eisenach, Frankfurt and Hamburg.

Telemann had a keen ear for the prevailing musical fashions and he made sure that his pieces were heard far and wide. He was one of the first composers to publish his vocal and instrumental music in a magazine format specifically targeted at amateur music-makers.

Although he was considered to be a real star in Germany during his lifetime, history has not judged

Telemann so kindly, and his musical contribution has been completely eclipsed by that of our next two composers – the undisputed kings of the Baroque period.

George Frideric Handel (1685–1759) and **Johann Sebastian Bach** (1685–1750) were born in Germany in the same year: 1685 was a very fine musical vintage indeed.

Johann Sebastian Bach had music in his blood. He was part of a German musical dynasty that spanned many generations, both before and after him. Some people believe that his music actually eclipses that of those two other giants of the classical music world – Mozart and Beethoven. Whatever the ranking, there is no doubt that Bach deserves to be among those considered as the greatest ever classical composers.

After he had died, there was a general reassessment of just how good a composer Bach really was and he gained the recognition that he deserved as a master of musical composition, particularly in the areas of choral, keyboard and instrumental works. There is a particularly strong spirituality to his music, which was influenced by Bach's dedicated religious faith.

By the time Johann Sebastian had reached double figures in age, both his parents had died. The young boy was sent to live with his older brother, Johann Christoph, who was, like their father, an organist.

Johann Christoph passed his skills on the organ to his younger brother. When Johann Sebastian was fifteen, he went away to a school 200 miles away and continued to study for another two years.

After leaving school, Johann Sebastian worked as a violinist before eventually taking up the family business and becoming an organist. One of the best-known stories about Bach concerns the lengths to which he would go to learn more about making music. On one occasion, when he was just nineteen, he made a 450-mile round trip on foot to hear a concert by his hero, the organist Dietrich Buxtehude.

In 1707, Bach married his cousin, Maria Barbara Bach. His first big job came a year later when he was appointed organist to the Duke of Saxe-Weimar. He stayed in the job for nine years, although his relationship with his boss became more than a little rocky towards the end of tenure, when he asked to leave for another job after being passed over for promotion. The Duke became so fed up with him that Bach was thrown in jail for a month. It wasn't the first time that Bach had fallen out with his employers; he had upset the Church authorities in one of his previous roles. He was definitely one of those people who reacted very badly to being told what to do.

In the end, Bach got his way and left to join the court of Prince Leopold of Anhalt-Cöthen as 'Kapellmeister' – the modern equivalent would be 'Director of Music'. Bach wrote much of his instrumental and orchestral music here. In 1720, his wife Maria died, but it didn't take Bach long to find a replacement, and his wedding to Anna Magdalena Wilcken took place just a year later.

In total, Bach had twenty children, although because of the high infant mortality rates at the time, only nine survived beyond their early childhood. Of these, Wilhelm Friedemann, Carl Philipp Emanuel, Johann Christoph Friedrich and Johann Christian all became composers.

Bach moved on to a job at a school in Leipzig in 1723, where he spent the final twenty-seven years of his life. It might come as a surprise now, but Bach was in fact the second choice for the job, with

Telemann being offered it first. As well as teaching, Bach was organist and choirmaster in the local church. He was required to create a huge number of choral pieces, and it was hard work. Once again, Bach fell out with the authorities, although this time he opted to stick with the job until the bitter end.

Among the many wonderful pieces Bach wrote during this period of his life, the two Easter works – the *St John Passion* and the *St Matthew Passion* – particularly stand out. On a more light-hearted note, he also wrote '*The Coffee Cantata*' for a music group that met in a local coffee house.

Bach always had a strong interest in maths and liked to represent numbers in his music. He believed that 14 was his own personal number because that was the total of his name scored when he added up the alphabetical position of each of its component letters. Patterns around the number 14 often appear in his music.

Towards the end of his life, Bach suffered from cataracts, and his eyesight began to fail. The English surgeon John Taylor botched an operation to cure the problem, just as he had done with Handel, and Bach was left almost totally blind. Just before Bach died something happened that corrected the problems with his eyes naturally, and for a short period he was able to see well enough to continue working on his final piece, *The Art of Fugue*.

Bach's rate of composition was quite remarkable, and after he died it took no fewer than forty-six years to collect and publish all his works.

Handel's father was not at all keen on his son taking up music as a career, and he banned the young boy from having anything to do with it, preferring him to study law before ending up with a sensible, secure job. Handel's mother, on the other hand, seemed to recognise talent when she heard it. History has it that she smuggled a small harpsichord into the attic of their home, where George Frideric would practise away, out of his father's earshot.

When Handel was eight years old, the Duke of Saxe-Weissenfels heard him play. The Duke was so impressed that he ensured that the boy had lessons. Such was Handel's natural talent that just three years later his tutor said that there was nothing left that he could teach him. Remarkably, this appears to have been the last time that Handel had formal music tuition; he was eleven.

In his late teens, Handel took up a role as an organist before moving to Hamburg, where he tried his hand at writing opera. He decided to move to Italy in order to improve that particular skill.

After around four years soaking up as much of the Italian music scene as he possibly could, Handel travelled to Hanover, where he was given a position in the court of the Elector.

The travel bug had well and truly bitten, though, and Handel asked for permission to visit England. His request was granted and he set off across the English Channel. Handel was a big hit in London, and his opera *Rinaldo* was greeted with universal acclaim – even though he had written it in just fifteen days. Although he did eventually return to Germany, Handel later travelled again to London, where he repeated his initial success.

By now, Handel was really pushing his luck as far as his employer was concerned. He was still on the payroll in Hanover, yet spent all his time away from the court. Suddenly, everything changed for him – and it was a change for the better.

The English monarch, Queen Anne, died. The heir to the throne was Handel's boss, the Elector of Hanover, who became King George I. The new King forgave Handel's absence, employing him in London. Handel must have felt at home in the city because this was the period when he wrote many of his greatest works, including his *Water Music*, which he composed in 1717 for a royal pageant on the River Thames.

In 1727, George I died and Handel continued to compose for George II, with *'Zadok the Priest'* written as a Coronation anthem. It has been sung at the Coronation of every British monarch ever since.

Handel's *Music for the Royal Fireworks* was composed for a display put on by King George II in London's Hyde Park. The music was a triumph, but the fireworks were an unmitigated disaster, with one particular catherine wheel setting fire to a wooden tower and causing pandemonium in the crowd.

One of Handel's most performed works today is his oratorio *Messiah*. It was written in aid of three Irish charities and was given its premiere in Dublin in 1741. It includes the incredibly uplifting *'Hallelujah Chorus'*, which is today heard regularly at Christmas and Easter. It was another example of how speedily Handel could produce the goods when required: even though the music lasts for two and a half hours, *Messiah* took him just twenty-four days to write.

Handel created the most incredible music and

was undoubtedly a complex character. He was grumpy, speaking English with a heavy accent and muttering constantly to himself in German; he had atrocious table manners and was a greedy eater.

Handel's success is a fine example of classical music's ability to cross geographical divides. Here was a man who was born in Germany yet became one of English music's greatest success stories, still being seen as part of the English Establishment centuries after his death. If you ever visit Westminster Abbey, make sure you pause to pay tribute to Handel: his body still lies there today.

When you talk about Scarlatti, make sure you refer to the right one. We're focusing on **Domenico Scarlatti** (1685–1757), rather than his lesser-known father, Alessandro.

Scarlatti was by no means as great a composer as the previous two giants of the Baroque period, with whom he shared the same birth year. He was, however, a fine keyboard player, and much of his best work was for the keyboard. Scarlatti wrote 500 or so sonatas for the instrument.

Legend suggests that Scarlatti once had a keyboard duel with Handel. The former played the harpsichord and the latter the organ. The judges appeared to have sat on the fence when it came to naming the winner: Scarlatti was declared the better harpsichordist and Handel the better organist.

Another contemporary of Handel – and yet another celebrated harpsichordist and organist – was the Frenchman **Jean-Philippe Rameau** (1683–1764). Born in Dijon, he travelled pretty much the length and breadth of France, with his fame at the time resting as much on his textbooks about music as it did on his composing and playing. Once he had settled permanently in Paris from 1722 onwards, he specialised in composing music for the stage. In his fifties, he rapidly inherited from Lully the position of being the most respected name in French opera. His pioneering work brought him to the attention of, first, the superbly named financier Alexandre le Riche de la Poupelinière (for whom he worked) and subsequently Louis XV himself. For the last two decades of his life he was the Royal Chamber Music Composer.

Our final composer from the Baroque period is one of the least well documented. He became more famous in South America than he ever did in his native Italy. **Domenico Zipoli** (1688–1726).

Born in Prato near Florence, where he studied, he began his successful career as a composer there, later working in Milan and Rome. Then, in 1716, he became a Jesuit missionary, sailing to Córdoba, Argentina, where he spent three years studying theology. He was part of the same so-called 'Jesuit Reductions' – an attempt to convert the local tribes to Christianity – that featured in the 1986 Roland Joffé movie *The Mission* (in which Father Gabriel soothes the locals with his exquisite oboe playing). His *Elevazione* has become a big favourite of Classic FM listeners. Two hundred years after his death, new repertoire by Zipoli was still being discovered. In the 1970s, around twenty previously unknown works turned up in Bolivia; he must have composed them while undertaking missionary work in Paraguay.

The End of the Baroque Period

Appropriately enough, Zipoli brings to an end our A-to-Z of composers from the Baroque period, which began back at the turn of the seventeenth century with Allegri. The Baroque composers marked 150 years of musical development. The influence of the Church at the end of the Baroque

period was far less marked than it was at the end of
the Early Music period. Kings, queens and noblemen were now major forces in commissioning new
music and employing musicians to perform it. This
was the period when classical music became showbiz – even though showbiz wouldn't be invented for
another couple of hundred years.

There were, however, still a huge number of
changes to come during the next period of classical
music – a time that many people regard as being at
the very heart of the whole genre.

Handy Baroque Playlist

1 Gregorio Allegri: *Miserere*
2 Orlando Gibbons: *This is the Record of John*
3 Jean-Baptiste Lully: *Alceste*
4 Marc-Antoine Charpentier: *Te Deum*
5 Arcangelo Corelli: *Concerto Grosso, Op. 6
No. 8*, known as *'The Christmas Concerto'*
6 Johann Pachelbel: *Canon in D*
7 Henry Purcell: *'When I Am Laid in Earth'*
known as *'Dido's Lament'*
8 Henry Purcell: The *Rondo* from *Abdelazar*
9 Henry Purcell: *Trumpet Tune and Air in D*
10 Henry Purcell: *'Come Ye Sons of Art'*

11   Jeremiah Clarke: *The Prince of Denmark's March*

12   Tomaso Albinoni: *Adagio in G minor*

13   Tomaso Albinoni: *Oboe Concerto in D minor, Op. 9 No. 2*

14   Antonio Vivaldi: *Four Seasons*

15   Antonio Vivaldi: *'Gloria'*

16   Antonio Vivaldi: *'Nulla in mundo pax sincera'*

17   Giuseppe Tartini: *Sonata in G minor for solo violin: 'The Devil's Trill'*

18   Georg Philipp Telemann: *Concerto in D for trumpet and strings*

19   Johann Sebastian Bach: *Brandenburg Concertos*

20   Johann Sebastian Bach: *Toccata and Fugue in D minor*

21   Johann Sebastian Bach: *St Matthew Passion*

22   Johann Sebastian Bach: *Goldberg Variations*

23   George Frideric Handel: *Messiah*

24   George Frideric Handel: *'Ombra mai fu'* from the opera *Xerxes*

25   George Frideric Handel: *'Zadok the Priest'*

26   George Frideric Handel: *Water Music*

27   George Frideric Handel: *Arrival of the Queen of Sheba* from the oratorio *Solomon*

28 Jean-Philippe Rameau: Overture to the
    ballet-opera *Les Indes galantes*
29 Domenico Scarlatti: *Sonata in A, K. 182*
30 Domenico Zipoli: *Elevazione*

three

The Classical Period

Isn't It All Classical?

In case you skipped the Preface to this book, this is a reminder that although everything we play on Classic FM is classical music, there was also a Classical period of classical music. It was neatly sandwiched between the Baroque period that we have just lived through, and the Romantic period, which is still to come. Broadly speaking, the Classical period runs from 1750 until 1830, so it is actually the shortest of all the periods that we cover.

Don't for a moment think that because this particular period spanned only eight decades, it was in any way light on new developments, big names or

stunning music. As you will see, it has all three by
the bucket-load.

As well as embracing the three classical greats
– Haydn, Mozart and Beethoven – the Classical
period also saw the development of the classical
symphony and concerto into the form that we would
regard as being normal today. More and more, composers were also being thought of as stars in their
own right, as classical music became a far wider
pursuit among the middle classes.

The musical changes of the Classical period
came about partly as a reaction to the Baroque
period that preceded it, and partly as a conse-
quence of the linear development of musical sound.
Mirroring a similar move in architecture, the musicians of the Classical period shifted from the ornate,
florid and intricate to the simple, clean-lined and
natural – directly reminiscent of the classicists.

What Else Was Going On in the World?

Scientific invention continued apace and the
Industrial Revolution arrived in Britain. Steam was
harnessed for the first time as a means of powering
large-scale factory production. James Hargreaves

came up with the 'Spinning Jenny', which revolutionised the cotton industry, and Benjamin Franklin invented the lightning conductor.

Big strides were made in the world of transport: James Brindley designed the Worsley-to-Manchester Canal; the first railway opened from Stockton to Darlington; and man flew for the very first time when two French brothers, Joseph and Jacques Montgolfier, created the first hot-air balloon in 1783.

James Cook discovered Australia and, not long afterwards, the first convicts started being shipped out. Meanwhile, America gained its independence and France underwent a revolution, which resulted in it losing its monarchy.

A Time of Change

Some of the composers in this chapter are extremely well known, others less so. Yet all influenced the development of the Classical period of classical music. Our first composer was one of those who started off working in the Baroque period, but ended up composing in Classical times. Steeped in the traditions of English choral music, **William Boyce** (1711–1779) was a boy chorister at St Paul's

Cathedral. He worked as an organist in London before becoming Composer to the Chapel Royal in 1736 and Master of the King's Musick in 1755. He was among the leading English composers of his generation, writing music for both the funeral of George II and the coronation of George III. Boyce had to retire from his musical posts in his sixties because of his increasing deafness.

It is for his contribution to the opera world that **Christoph Willibald von Gluck** (1714–1787) is best remembered today. This German cellist and composer was lucky enough to spend his formative years fairly loaded down with princely patrons, who paid his way. He studied in Milan and developed a penchant for opera around this time, becoming much in demand as a composer. By the 1750s, he started to develop the idea of enhancing the drama in operas, as well as the singing. The reform did not always go down well with the divas on the stage, but it was a huge step forward in the history of opera and set a new benchmark for the composers who followed him.

Just as Purcell and Monteverdi had done before him, Gluck took the story of Orpheus and Euridice and turned it into an opera. His style was very different from that of previous composers, with greater emphasis on characterisation and storytelling. He also included two sections of ballet in the opera, including *The Dance of the Blessed Spirits*, which remains very popular today.

Gluck cleaned opera up from being a vehicle for star singers to show off to one that allowed the story to shine through. He was among the first composers to use clarinets, cors anglais (they look like oversized oboes) and trombones in his operas.

Gluck died in Vienna after suffering a series of strokes. It is believed that his death was brought on by his insistence on drinking an after-dinner liqueur, even though his doctor had forbidden him to do so.

Carl Philipp Emanuel Bach (1714–1788) was born in the same year as Gluck. You would, of course, be right in thinking that the name sounds familiar. Carl Philipp Emanuel Bach was the son of Johann Sebastian Bach. Although he was nowhere near as important a composer as his father, Carl Philipp Emanuel did make a significant contribution to the development of the Classical sound, acting as a bridge between the Baroque style encapsulated by Johann Sebastian and the clearly different Classical style of composers such as Haydn and Mozart – of whom, more in a moment. Carl Philipp Emanuel's earliest works sounded very much like those of his father, whereas his later works were more similar to Haydn's.

During his lifetime, Carl Philipp Emanuel was famous as a keyboard player, working for King Frederick the Great for some twenty-eight years. As a composer, he developed the sound of the sonata. He took over from Telemann as music director in Hamburg, where he was in charge of around 200 performances a year in five different churches. Carl Philipp Emanuel managed to find time to write a manual called *The Art of Keyboard Playing*, which was used by many of the pianists who followed him. As his name is such a mouthful, you'll also hear him referred to as C. P. E. Bach.

Joseph Haydn (1732–1809) was one of the great architects of the Classical period. He lived longer than many of his contemporaries and witnessed huge developments in the way that music was written during his seventy-seven-year life. Haydn was particularly influential in developing the symphony, sonata and string quartet, and was to become a major inspiration to those who followed him, including Mozart and Beethoven.

Haydn was another man with a tremendous creative urge, publishing around 1,200 works, including no fewer than 104 symphonies, more than 80 string quartets, over 50 piano sonatas, at least 24 concertos and 20 operas. Then there are nearly 90 choral works, more than 100 songs, plus literally hundreds of other pieces for solo instruments or chamber groups, all of which bore Haydn's name.

Born in the year that London's first Royal Opera House opened for business, Haydn was showing amazing musical talent by the time he was just five years old. Three years later, he became a choirboy at St Stephen's Cathedral in Venice. Back in Haydn's day, castrati were still relatively common. These were men, who, without putting too fine a point on it, had been operated on to ensure that their voices never actually broke. Haydn had a magnificent singing voice as a boy and his choirmaster suggested he could keep it for ever if he would just undergo a very small operation. Haydn was happy to go along with the idea, until his horrified father found out what was about to happen and the boy was told what the operation would actually entail.

Haydn was able to compose so much principally because of the patronage of the Esterházy family, who were extremely influential within Hungarian society. At the age of twenty-nine he was given a job by Prince Paul Esterházy and he remained in the family's service for the next three decades. He also became one of the first truly international musical figures, making tours around Europe, in the way that Take That or Coldplay might do today. Haydn was particularly popular on his visits to England, and he had two long stays in the country at the end of his life. This allowed him to build up quite a treasure chest of riches – he was most certainly not the stereotypical impoverished composer we shall meet so often in this book.

Haydn's success is all the more remarkable because he appears, in the main, to have taught himself about music. This seems to have been a benefit rather than a drawback, allowing him to develop his own style of composing, free from the constraints of the perceived wisdoms of the time.

It is for his symphonies that Haydn is most remembered today. Many of them were given nicknames, with fun stories attached as to how they got those names.

Take the *'Farewell'* – *Symphony No. 45* – for example. This was composed while Haydn was working for the Esterházy family. The court musicians were fed up with being separated from their wives and families. Haydn wanted to get the message across to his boss, so the musical score instructed the musicians one by one to blow out the candles by their music stands and exit the stage. At the end, only the two principal violinists are left.

The nicknames go on, including the *'Clock' Symphony (No. 101)*, so called because of the tick-tocking slow movement, and the *'Surprise' Symphony (No. 94)*, with its deadening chord that comes crashing in after a very quiet opening. There are many others too: *'Philosopher'*, *'Mercury'*, *'Schoolmaster'*, *'Bear'*, *'Hen'*, *'Miracle'*, and a whole group known as the *'London Symphonies'*.

Other Classical Players

During his lifetime, **Johann Christian Bach** (1735–1782) was far more famous than his father, Johann Sebastian, had been in his. Johann Christian's claim to fame was that he was the first person to give a solo piano performance in London, and he is sometimes referred to as the 'London Bach'.

Johann Christian made a lot of money early on

his career, but things went wrong for him financially towards the end of his life and his reputation started to wane.

Karl Ditters von Dittersdorf (1739–1799) appears in this book not because he was by any means the most influential or creative composer of the Classical period. In fact, many histories of classical music don't include him at all. He is here as an act of self-indulgence because of his wonderful name, which has become a great favourite with Classic FM presenters over the years.

Now largely forgotten, he was actually one of the most popular composers in Europe during his lifetime, although he never managed to turn that popularity into financial stability. He wrote more than 120 symphonies and 45 operas, as well as choral and chamber works. His music deserves to have a wider hearing and, with a name like that, he might just catch the listening public's imagination once again.

He might have written around 600 different works, but **Luigi Boccherini** (1743–1805) is famous today for one piece in particular – the 'Minuet' from his *String Quintet in E*, which featured in the British cinema classic *The Ladykillers*. In fact, he actually wrote no fewer than 154 different quintets for various combinations of instruments.

During his lifetime, Boccherini was a star performer on the cello, touring Italy, France and Spain. His life ended unhappily, though. He outlived his two wives and several of his children and was himself unwell for some years, before eventually dying in poverty. Had he lived just a few years longer, Boccherini would have seen his music coming back into fashion.

Our next composer is more famous today for a crime he did not commit, rather than for the music he wrote. However, for more than five decades the Italian composer and conductor **Antonio Salieri** (1750–1825) was one of the most influential forces in the Viennese musical world. He enjoyed great success as an opera composer in Italy and France. Towards the end of his life, he concentrated on teaching.

Depending on your point of view, Salieri was either done a great disservice, or his place in history was secured by Pushkin's 1831 play *Mozart and Salieri* and Peter Schaffer's stunning 1979 play *Amadeus*, which became an equally stunning 1984 film of the same name.

To find out why, we need look no further than our next composer.

The Classical Big Hitters

The argument rages between Mozart and Beethoven fans: which one was truly the greatest? The composer who appears to be in the ascendant at any given moment tends to depend on who has celebrated a significant anniversary most recently. If we look to the Classic FM Hall of Fame for help, then we find that Mozart consistently has more entries in the Top 300 than Beethoven, but a greater number of Beethoven's works tend to be clustered more towards the higher echelons of the chart. So with honours fairly even between the two, there is little doubt in our minds at Classic FM that, along with Johann Sebastian Bach, Mozart and Beethoven are the true giants of classical music composition.

Johannes Chrysostomus Wolfgangus Amadeus Mozart (1756–1791) was born in Salzburg on a snowy evening in January 1756. He was an incredible child prodigy, playing the piano at the age of three and composing by the time he was just four years old.

His father **Leopold Mozart** (1719–1787)

was a composer and violinist, and a member of the orchestra belonging to the Prince-Archbishop of Salzburg. In 1762, he was promoted to court composer. His talent was nowhere near as great as that of his son, but music appears to have been in the Mozart family's blood, and Wolfgang's sister, Maria Anna (known as Nannerl), was a fine pianist.

When Leopold realised just how gifted his children were, he decided to take them on a tour of Europe. It was an epic journey that lasted for four years, taking in Munich, Vienna, Paris, London, Amsterdam, Munich again, and finally Salzburg.

Mozart was just six when the tour began and by its end he was a star, having played in front of the most influential people wherever he had been. Throughout his life, Mozart was a keen letter-writer and many of his notes to friends and family survive today, giving us an authentic glimpse into his life.

As a child, Mozart learned fast how to wow an audience and could do all sorts of tricks at the piano. One of his favourites was to play with his hands hidden under a cloth, so that he was unable to see any of the notes. But he didn't just excel at performing; by the time he was twelve years old, he had already completed two operas.

It was time for Mozart to get back on the road again. On this occasion, the destination was Italy. The story goes that he heard a performance of Allegri's *Miserere* (see page 25). By papal decree, no printed parts existed for this work outside the confines of the Vatican. The young Mozart was so moved by the piece, though, that he rushed off and scribbled the whole work down on to manuscript paper, note perfect. This was a feat of pure musical genius. Although this particular tale is almost certainly apocryphal, it none the less bears repeating, as it's very much part of the Mozart legend.

While he was in Italy, Mozart was fascinated by the native opera composers and, by the end of his life, he himself had written some of the greatest examples of the genre, including *The Marriage of Figaro*, *Don Giovanni*, *Così fan tutte* and *The Magic Flute*.

Joseph Haydn was one of the great musical influences on Mozart's career, and each man was an unashamed fan of the other's work. Haydn told Mozart's father: 'I must tell you before God and as an honest man, that your son is the greatest composer I ever heard of.'

As a teenager, Mozart began working for the

Prince Archbishop of Salzburg. It was always destined to be a troubled relationship, which culminated years later in Mozart literally being kicked out of the job with a boot up his backside.

Mozart spent his early years being lauded as a genius, and this took its toll on his relationships with those around him. He could be incredibly arrogant, and went through his life exhibiting a talent for upsetting people and for making enemies.

In love, Mozart was both pragmatic and persistent. When a young lady called Aloysia Weber spurned his advances, he turned his attention to her sister, Constanze, instead. A year later, they were married and they went on to have children of their own. They stayed together for the rest of Mozart's life in a very strong and loving marriage.

Some composers need to spend hours working and reworking every note that they write, but Mozart was a very speedy composer, creating intensely tuneful melodies from scratch, seemingly plucking them out of the air at every turn. Once, when he was walking along the street, a beggar asked him for some money. Instead of tossing him a coin, he wrote out a tune on a piece of manuscript paper, telling the beggar to take it to a music publisher, who would exchange it for cash. Mozart himself said: 'I write as a sow piddles.'

Mozart was terrible when it came to looking after his finances. He worked hard and earned well for many years, but no matter how fast the money came in, he would always spend more than he had. During his final years, he was heavily in debt to many of his friends, who had no hope of ever seeing their loans again.

In the final year of his life, Mozart's health gradually deteriorated and there are all sorts of conspiracy theories about how Mozart came to die, including the idea that he was murdered by Antonio Salieri (as suggested in the play *Mozart and Salieri* and the film and play *Amadeus*). The story goes that a 'masked stranger' came to Mozart's door and commissioned him to write a requiem. The shadowy figure at the door was not in fact Salieri, but was instead a servant of a nobleman, who probably intended to pass off Mozart's work as his own. Mozart began to believe that the 'masked stranger' was the Devil himself and that the requiem was in fact for his own death. As he worked on the piece, his health worsened and he never managed to finish it. The final parts were completed by his pupil, Süssmayr.

Mozart left his finances in a parlous state when he died at the tragically young age of thirty-five. He was buried in an unmarked grave just outside Vienna, leaving behind more than 650 different works, which showed his mastery of every type of classical music. Opera, symphonies, concertos, chamber works, choral pieces: whatever he turned his hand to, Mozart could write with aplomb. It was a sad end to a truly great composer's life.

Mozart was a great letter writer and his surviving correspondence spans a twenty-two-year period from his teens to just before his death, forming one of the most amazing non-musical legacies of any composer. What they reveal very much counterbalances the traditional portrait of an angelic genius. The Mozart of the letters is coarse, rude, childish and apparently badly schooled in grammar (no doubt partly to do with his touring childhood). His obsession with his own, and others', nether regions is undeniable and, while their reading might make some uncomfortable, they show a very 'humanising' side to a great mind. Comments such as the one written while he was composing *The Magic Flute*

– 'Today, out of absolute tedium, I wrote an aria for the opera' – serve to shed light on Mozart the man, possibly helping us to appreciate him all the more.

It seems strange to have the two biggest names in classical music side by side in this book. It has not happened by design and is purely an accident of their dates of birth. However, in many people's view, the pinnacle of classical music appears in these few pages covering the lives of Mozart and Beethoven. They might have a point, although there are plenty of gems still to come.

You might remember that, earlier on, we discussed the rather inexact science of deciding exactly where a period of classical music starts and where it ends. Well, Beethoven's music is a case in point, with his life straddling the end of the Classical period and the beginning of the Romantic period that followed. To illustrate this, it's worth looking at his symphonies as an example. His *Symphony No. 1* very much follows the form of those Classical symphonies written by Haydn and Mozart, but by the time his *Symphony No. 9* was premiered, Beethoven was writing music that sounded very different indeed.

Ludwig van Beethoven (1770–1827) liked to claim that the 'van' in the middle of his name meant that he came from noble stock, but in fact he was descended from a perfectly normal family, with his ancestors originally coming from Holland.

There is no doubt that Beethoven had a tough childhood, though, and he was often beaten by his alcoholic father. He had obvious musical talent and his father was determined that he would become the 'new Mozart'.

As a teenager, he was appointed as court organist in Bonn. When he was sixteen, he travelled to Vienna to play for Mozart, who was fourteen years older. Mozart was impressed, saying: 'Keep your eye on him; one day he will make the world talk of him.' He agreed to take on the teenager as a pupil, creating one of the great 'what ifs?' of classical music. Shortly after their meeting, Beethoven was called back home to Bonn to look after his sick mother. As a result, the lessons with Mozart never took place, but musicologists through the years have spent many hours wondering what might have transpired had they gone ahead.

Around the time of Beethoven's twentieth birthday, he met Haydn, who offered to give him lessons in Vienna. Beethoven took up the opportunity and settled in the city for the rest of his life, quickly gaining the reputation as the best keyboard player in town.

Haydn said of his pupil: 'This young man will in time fill the position of one of Europe's greatest composers, and I shall be proud to be able to speak of myself as his teacher.'

Unfortunately, Beethoven could be every bit as arrogant as Mozart – if not worse. He said Haydn was a teacher 'from whom I learned absolutely nothing'.

In his twenties, Beethoven began to have trouble with his hearing, and by his forties he was completely deaf. He continued to create works of outstanding musicality and originality, without ever being able to hear a single note played. It is one of the most remarkable achievements in this whole book, and Beethoven should be marked as one of the very greatest classical composers for that reason alone. Yet Beethoven does not need to be shown any favours because of his disability. The music he created has stood the test of time and is regarded as among the greatest of the entire classical repertoire.

Although Beethoven refused to be defeated by his deafness, he did have trouble coming to terms with it. He would angrily thump the piano in an effort to hear the notes, sometimes even breaking the strings inside. He became an increasingly difficult person to be around, often drinking heavily, and he began to look increasingly unkempt, with wild hair and scruffy clothes.

Just as Mozart had done before him, Beethoven mastered a wide range of different types of classical music: from concertos to choral works, and from string quartets to pieces for solo instruments. He was a great concert pianist and wrote with an absolute understanding of what the instrument could achieve. Beethoven's best-known work for solo piano, the 'Moonlight' Sonata, wasn't given the name by Beethoven himself, acquiring it instead from a critic, who thought that the piece evoked an image of the moon over Lake Lucerne.

Unlike Mozart, Beethoven tended to take a long time to write each of his pieces. Mozart was able to dash off a new work incredibly quickly, whereas Beethoven liked to spend ages working on a new tune. He would often work things out in his head before finally writing it down. Then he would spend a long time crossing things out and trying new ideas before eventually settling on what he wanted.

Beethoven composed only one opera – *Fidelio* – and it took him years to get it right. He rewrote one aria no fewer than eighteen times and came up with four different overtures before he settled on one that he liked.

Beethoven's speciality was the symphony – the style of which he developed hugely during his lifetime. For many, his final symphony – *No. 9* – was his biggest triumph, with a much larger orchestra, choir and four soloists. It includes the magnificent final movement, the '*Ode to Joy*'.

By the time this piece was first performed in public, Beethoven was completely deaf. On the big night, he stood on stage with his back to the audience. At the end of the concert, it was only when one of the singers turned him around to face the crowd that he realised that they had been wildly cheering and applauding his masterpiece.

Beethoven was fifty-six years old when he died, after making tentative sketches for a tenth symphony. His funeral was very different from that of Mozart. More than 30,000 people came out on to the streets to say goodbye. His torch-bearers included Franz Schubert – of whom more later.

Beethoven was a musical innovator. He led a troubled private life and never married, even though he fell hopelessly in love with a series of women. Often his passion was unrequited. He dedicated his *Bagatelle in A minor*, which was composed in 1810, to 'Elise' – although his handwriting was so bad that musical historians believe he might actually have intended to dedicate it to Therese Malfatti, the wife of his doctor. His publisher is said to have misread the dedication, perhaps meaning that one of the most famous of all Beethoven's works ended up being a musical love letter to an 'Elise' who never actually existed. In addition to the problems caused by his deafness, Beethoven often had an unhappy time of it and regularly became consumed with anger – particularly over a long-running custody battle with the mother of the son of his dead brother. Listening to music such as the *'Moonlight' Sonata*, this seems hard to believe. But sadly it is true.

Our final composer from the Classical period is almost completely eclipsed by Mozart and Beethoven, but nevertheless he was still an

innovator in his own way. In fact, **Louis Spohr**
(1784–1859) was something of a revolutionary on
the quiet. Born in Braunschweig, he soon outgrew
infant-prodigy status to tour Russia and Germany as
both violinist and conductor. As well as being one
of the first conductors to use a baton to keep time,
he also invented the chin rest for the violin, some
time around 1820.

Not only was he a well-respected composer,
but Spohr was also a brilliant violinist in his day.
He was widely admired as a teacher and his book,
Violin Tutor, became required reading. Spohr was
another of those composers whose output had one
foot in the Classical period and the other in the
Romantic period.

The End of the Classical Period

It might be the shortest period we cover in this
book; however, this was a time that was by no
means lacking in stature or importance in the overall development of classical music. The Classical
years were marked out by some of the true greats.
For the first time, composers became star names in
their own right and, by the start of our next period,
classical music had changed beyond all recognition

from the style and forms that were the norms at the end of the Baroque period just eighty years before.

Handy Classical Playlist

1 William Boyce: *Symphony No. 4*
2 Christoph Willibald von Gluck: *The Dance of the Blessed Spirits* from *Orpheus and Euridice*
3 C. P. E. Bach: *Harpsichord Concerto in D minor*
4 C. P. E. Bach: *Magnificat*
5 Joseph Haydn: *The Creation*
6 Joseph Haydn: *Symphony No. 101 ('The Clock')*
7 Joseph Haydn: *Cello Concertos Nos 1* and 2
8 Joseph Haydn: *The Seasons*
9 J. C. Bach: *Symphonies, Op. 3*
10 Karl Ditters von Dittersdorf: *Harp Concerto*
11 Luigi Boccherini: *String Quintet in E*
12 Luigi Boccherini: *Cello Concerto No. 9*
13 Antonio Salieri: *Flute and Oboe Concerto*
14 Leopold Mozart: *Toy Symphony*
15 Wolfgang Amadeus Mozart: *'Laudate Dominum'*
16 Wolfgang Amadeus Mozart: *Requiem*

17 Wolfgang Amadeus Mozart: *Clarinet Concerto*

18 Wolfgang Amadeus Mozart: *Piano Concerto No. 21*

19 Wolfgang Amadeus Mozart: *Horn Concerto No. 4*

20 Wolfgang Amadeus Mozart: *Serenade No. 13 ('Eine kleine Nachtmusik')*

21 Wolfgang Amadeus Mozart: *Symphony No. 41 ('Jupiter')*

22 Wolfgang Amadeus Mozart: *Così fan tutte*

23 Wolfgang Amadeus Mozart: *Don Giovanni*

24 Wolfgang Amadeus Mozart: *The Magic Flute*

25 Wolfgang Amadeus Mozart: *The Marriage of Figaro*

26 Ludwig van Beethoven: *Symphony No. 5*

27 Ludwig van Beethoven: *Symphony No. 6 ('Pastoral')*

28 Ludwig van Beethoven: *Symphony No. 9 ('Choral')*

29 Ludwig van Beethoven: *Piano Sonata No. 14 ('Moonlight')*

30 Ludwig van Beethoven: *Bagatelle in A minor ('Für Elise')*

31 Ludwig van Beethoven: *Violin Concerto*

32 Ludwig van Beethoven: *Piano Concerto No. 5*
    ('Emperor')

33 Ludwig van Beethoven: *Fidelio*

34 Louis Spohr: *Clarinet Concerto No. 1*

four

The Early Romantics

Why Romantic?

The Romantic period of classical music ran from around 1830 to 1910 or so, although the dates are frequently disputed. As with many labels used in this book, a strict definition of why Romantic music is romantic is quite hard to come by. There are parts of music written in all of the periods we cover that could be considered to be 'romantic'.

The composers whose work falls into this category tend to bring emotions to the fore in their music, and often use the notes they write to paint pictures in a very expressive way. This is different from those composers who came before them in the Classical period. For them, writing music tended to be about having a formal structure, or framework, within which to compose.

Having said all of this, there are composers from the Classical period who have elements of Romanticism in their music, just as there are composers from the Romantic period who have elements of Classicism in their music. Really, there is no hard and fast rule, just a series of general indicators.

What Else Was Going On in the World?

History didn't stand still just because everyone was going all Romantic. Inventions during this period included socialism, postage stamps and the Salvation Army. Vitamins and radium were discovered; the Suez Canal opened; Mr Daimler produced his first motorcar, and the Wright brothers flew in their flying machine. Radio was born when Marconi successfully sent a message by wireless to a receiver over a mile away; Queen Victoria celebrated her jubilee, and the Great Gold Rush got under way.

The Three Ages of the Romantics

As you flick through this book, you might notice that this period is the most substantial by far, with no fewer than seventy-three composers included across three different chapters. Much of the music was composed in different countries simultaneously and many of the composers' lives overlapped. To keep things as clear as possible, we have divided this era into three groups of composers: the Early Romantics, the Nationalist Romantics and the Late Romantics.

The Early Romantics

These are the composers who bridged the gap between the Classical period and the later Romantic period. Many of them were alive at the same time as the Classical composers, and they were certainly influenced by the likes of Mozart and Beethoven. However, all of them moved the development of classical music on in their own way.

Our first composer from the Romantic period was already wowing the crowds in his home city of Dublin by the time he was ten years old. So much so that his father took the young **John Field** (1782–1837) off to London to seek his fame and fortune. There, he studied with the piano genius **Muzio Clementi** (1752–1832) and just got better and better. Field always saw himself as a pianist who composed, rather than purely as a composer. He travelled around Europe playing Clementi's compositions, ultimately settling in St Petersburg. He developed a series of twenty short pieces for the piano, which he called 'nocturnes'. As we shall see a bit later, this idea was taken up and developed by Chopin, who became famous for his nocturnes, but it was actually Field who invented the genre.

The child superstars just keep on coming around this time and even in a period stuffed with musical prodigies, **Niccolò Paganini** (1782–1840) appears to have been something of a wonder and he was a superstar in his lifetime. During his performances, he was the consummate showman, able to perform all sorts of stunts using his violin. In the same way that Jimi Hendrix could amaze audiences more than a century later as a rock guitar virtuoso, Paganini was able to stun those who saw him perform with his outrageously good playing and his phenomenal technique had firmly established him as a great solo artist by the time he was twenty-seven.

Paganini could play complete works with just two strings on his violin instead of four. Sometimes, he would even deliberately snap some of the strings mid-performance – and still play the piece brilliantly.

Paganini's childhood was completely centred on music, and his father would punish him for not practising by withdrawing food and water. As an adult, Paganini's playing was so good that there were even stories suggesting that the only way anybody could possibly play the violin that well was if they had entered into a pact with the Devil. When he died, the Church initially refused to allow Paganini's body to be buried on its land for this reason.

Paganini was in no doubt about the benefits of being seen as a showman, saying, 'I am not handsome, but when women hear me play, they come crawling to my feet.'

The style and structure of music was continuing to change in the operatic world, just as it was in music written for instrumentalists. In Germany, **Carl Maria von Weber** (1786–1826) was at the vanguard of developments, although he lived outside the years that many people consider to be the Romantic period.

Opera was the family business as far as Weber was concerned, and he spent his childhood touring with the opera company that his father had set up. He was taught by Haydn's brother, Michael, in Salzburg and also studied for a time in Vienna. A productive period in Stuttgart was halted by seemingly false charges of financial fraud, whereupon he embarked on a period of short-term conducting jobs in Darmstadt, Munich, Prague and Dresden.

It was in Dresden that he wrote his opera *Der Freischütz*, which sealed his place in German musical history because of its use of folk tunes in the score. You will see a little later that this is an idea that became increasingly common in the Romantic period.

Weber also wrote a couple of cracking clarinet concertos – and it is for these that he is chiefly remembered today. He died from tuberculosis at the age of just thirty-nine while rehearsing his *Oberon* for its premiere at Covent Garden.

Italy is the home of opera and in **Gioachino Rossini** (1792–1868) the Italians had a new hero. He wrote both comic and tragic operas to equal acclaim.

His parents originally intended Rossini to become a blacksmith, despite having a singer for a mother and a wayward horn player for a father. At the age of fourteen, however, he was enrolled in the Music Academy of Bologna; four years later, he wrote his first full-scale opera, one of the staggering total of thirty-nine he composed during his career.

Rossini was another of those composers who created new works very quickly, and it never seemed to take him longer than a few weeks to write an opera. At the height of his creative powers, he once said: 'Give me a laundry list and I will set it to music.' Rossini claimed to have composed the whole of *The Barber of Seville* in just thirteen days. His fast work rate meant that he had a stream of new operas premiering in opera houses across Italy. He did not always get on well with the interpreters of his creations, though, saying, 'How wonderful the opera world would be if there were no singers.'

Rossini married the soprano Isabella Colbran when he was thirty, after which he began to travel more. He met Beethoven in Vienna – according to Rossini, the German composer made disparaging comments about Italians – and he also visited Britain. He settled, though, in Paris, where he composed *William Tell*, his grandest and longest operatic work.

Then, at the age of thirty-seven, Rossini suddenly stopped writing opera altogether, and in the final three decades of his life his only major work was the choral piece *Stabat Mater*. It's never been quite clear why he decided to do this, although by then his bank balance was particularly healthy following on from his enormous critical and financial successes around Europe.

Aside from the music, Rossini was a great lover of food and his name has been appended to more dishes than any other composer. Omelette Rossini and Salade Rossini sit alongside the ubiquitous Tournedos Rossini on menus. In case you're wondering, the last dish is made from steak layered on croutons with foie gras and truffles on top.

Born into a close-knit Sicilian family, **Vincenzo Bellini** (1801–1835) was said to have been singing operatic arias by the time he was eighteen months old. The success of two of his early operas, *Il Pirata* and *La Straniera*, propelled him to centre stage in the Italian operatic world. He cited Rossini as a great influence on his work and, at the height of his success, was matching him in terms of financial earnings.

Bellini was one of those composers who relied on a deadline to get his creative juices flowing. He had many lovers in his life, including the famous soprano Giuditta Pasta, who created the role of Norma in Bellini's opera of the same name. Sadly, Bellini died very young. Rossini was one of the pall-bearers at his funeral in Paris.

Our next composer was another who sadly didn't live as long as he might have hoped. Now, he did like to party the night away as much as the next chap, but he was by no means a slacker when it came to doing his day job.

He may have lived for only thirty-one years, but **Franz Schubert** (1797–1828) was a highly proficient composer by the time he was seventeen, and he still managed to leave behind more than 600 songs (known as 'Lieder'). Schubert also composed 8½ symphonies, 11 operas and around 400 other pieces. In 1815 alone, he composed 144 songs, two Masses, a symphony and a selection of other works.

In 1815, he wrote *'Gretchen am Spinnrade'* (*'Gretchen at the spinning-wheel'*), *'Der Erlkönig'* (*'The Earl King'*) and many other great songs, plus two more symphonies, three Masses and four stage works. It was a remarkable display of creativity by any standards. 'I compose every morning', Schubert once said, 'and when one piece is done, I begin another.'

All that composing didn't prevent Schubert from having a good time and he was famous for his musical parties, or 'Schubertiads', as they were known.

Schubert contracted syphilis in 1823 and died of typhus five years later in 1828. A year earlier, he had taken part in the funeral of his great hero Ludwig van Beethoven.

Interestingly, Schubert was one of the first major composers to rely on other people to promulgate his music. He himself only ever gave one major concert, in the year of his death, and this was overshadowed by Paganini, who had arrived in Vienna at the same time. So poor old Schubert was never really given the credit he deserved in his lifetime or in the years that followed his death.

One of the great mysteries of Schubert's life is his *Symphony No. 8*, which is known as the *'Unfinished' Symphony*. He completed the first two movements, and then abandoned it. Nobody is quite sure why, but it still remains one of his most popular works today.

Hector Berlioz's (1803–1869) father was a doctor, and Berlioz didn't receive the sort of hot-housed musical education favoured by the parents of many of the other composers in this book.

Berlioz actually began to train in Paris as a doctor himself, but ended up spending more and more time sneaking off to the opera. In the end, he switched courses to study music, much to his family's disgust.

Berlioz was almost a caricature of how non-composers think a composer should be: very highly strung with frequent temper tantrums; recklessly impulsive; capable of being intensely passionate, and, of course, absolutely hopelessly romantic when it came to falling in love. He once pursued an ex-lover with pistols and poison; he followed another disguised as a maid.

The principal object of Berlioz's desires was an actress called Harriet Smithson, whom he chased with a dedication that must have seriously unnerved her. He first saw her in a play in 1827, but didn't actually meet her until 1832. At first, she spurned his advances, and he wrote his *Symphonie fantastique* as a response. They were finally married in 1833, but – true to form – he fell hopelessly in love with someone else within a few years.

When it came to writing music, Berlioz was not

afraid to think big. Take his *Requiem*, for example. It was written for a huge orchestra and chorus, as well as four brass bands, one at each corner of the stage. It was the same when he was putting on concerts of other people's works, too. On one legendary occasion, he conducted a performance of Beethoven's *Symphony No. 5* with no fewer than thirty-six double-basses in the orchestra.

This addiction to making everything as big as possible has not always stood Berlioz in good stead since his death. It means that it can be prohibitively expensive to stage his works in the way that he envisaged them because of the vast number of musicians who have to be paid. He knew his own mind, though, and composed with zeal, saying, 'Every composer knows the anguish and despair occasioned by forgetting ideas which one has no time to write down.'

Anyone reading this book, who has not yet left school, would be forgiven for feeling a pang of jealousy when they come across the likes of **Felix Mendelssohn** (1809–1847). He was, as we have seen before in these pages, and will see again before the end of our story, a child prodigy.

Mendelssohn didn't just excel at music, though;

he was one of those infuriating individuals who seem to be brilliant at just about anything they try: painting, poetry, sport, languages – he mastered them all.

Mendelssohn was lucky in that he was born into a wealthy family who were part of Berlin's 'arty set'. During his childhood, Mendelssohn met many of the city's most talented artists and musicians in his own home.

Mendelssohn made his public debut at the age of nine and by the time he was sixteen he had composed his *Octet* for strings. A year later he wrote his overture to Shakespeare's *A Midsummer Night's Dream*. It would be another seventeen years before Mendelssohn would complete the rest of his incidental music for the same play (including the *'Wedding March'*, which is a feature of many marriage services today).

Mendelssohn was a cultured man with a happy, stable marriage and five children. He worked hard and travelled widely, including to Scotland. He didn't seem to think too much of the place, saying. '[They] brew nothing but whisky, fog and foul weather.'

This did not stop him from writing two of his

most loved works about the country. His *'Scottish'
Symphony* was composed thirteen years after his
first trip there, and his *Hebrides Overture* is based
in some parts on Scottish folk tunes.

Mendelssohn had other links to Britain, with his
oratorio *Elijah* receiving its premiere in Birmingham
in 1846. He even became friendly with Queen
Victoria, and was Prince Albert's piano teacher for
a short while.

As well as being a composer, Mendelssohn was
a respected conductor. He became Music Director
of the Leipzig Gewandhaus Orchestra at the age
of only twenty-six. He also founded a major music
school in the city, persuading his fellow composers
Ignaz Moscheles and Robert Schumann to join him
on the staff.

Mendelssohn died at the tragically young age
of thirty-eight. There was no question that he was
pushing himself to the limit and was working too
hard, but he never really got over the death of
his beloved sister, Fanny, who was also a gifted
musician.

Here is another character who was a Romantic
through and through. **Frédéric Chopin** (1810–
1849) showed a dedication to one musical

instrument, the like of which we see nowhere else in this book.

To say that Chopin loved the piano would be an understatement. He adored it, dedicating his life to taking piano composition and performance to new heights. In fact, he wrote virtually nothing else of note for any other instrument at all, other than when an orchestra was involved in a supporting role to a piano soloist.

Chopin was born in 1810 in Warsaw, to a French father and Polish mother. By the time he was just seven years old, he was already composing and performing; he never looked back. After studying at the Warsaw Conservatoire during his teenage years, he went on the road in 1830, giving concerts in cities as far apart as Dresden, Prague, Vienna and Stuttgart before travelling on to Paris.

Chopin became a fixture in Paris society, making good money by teaching rich people how to play the piano. He was fastidious about how he looked and always careful to ensure that he was wearing the most fashionable outfits.

As a composer, Chopin was particularly methodical. Not for him a hurried scribbling out of a new piece. Instead, composition was a rather painful and drawn-out process. He ended up writing 169 works for solo piano, and each one was finessed to perfection.

Chopin fell in love with a celebrated French writer with the remarkable name Amandine-Aurore-Lucile Dupin. She is better known under her male pseudonym, George Sand. She certainly sounds like a bit of a character. She could often be seen strutting about the streets of Paris wearing men's clothes and smoking a large cigar, much to the shock of polite society in the French capital. Chopin and Sand had a stormy relationship and eventually fell out of love.

Chopin was another of the Romantic composers who died young, claimed by tuberculosis at the age of thirty-nine, shortly after his relationship with Sand broke up.

Robert Schumann (1810–1856) was yet another composer whose life was a tale of tragedy and early death. He was a brilliant composer, but spent most of his life in the shadow of his wife **Clara Schumann** (1819–1896), who was one of the most famed pianists of the day. She was less well known as a composer, but wrote highly attractive music.

Schumann was born in Zwickau, some fifty miles south of Leipzig and not far from the Czech border. When he was nineteen, Schumann began taking piano lessons from Friedrich Wieck, and began pursuing the hand of Clara Wieck, totally against the wishes of her father. Determined not to be beaten, Schumann went to court to fight Wieck's objections to the marriage, but, in the end, the couple had to wait until she was old enough to marry without her father's consent.

They were blissfully happy together, although Schumann was unable to follow his dream of becoming a concert pianist because of an injury to his hand, and he was not always happy to live in the shadow of his wife's celebrity.

He is best remembered today for his piano pieces, his songs and his chamber music. Schumann suffered from syphilis and depression, trying to commit suicide by throwing himself into the River Rhine. He was placed in an asylum, where he died two years later.

Schumann was pragmatic about his art, saying, 'In order to compose, all you have to do is remember a tune that nobody else thought of.'

Clara Schumann must have been a formidable woman. She resolutely fought her father when it came to her marriage to Robert, and stuck by her husband until his sad end. At this point, she became the chief interpreter of his music, bringing it to as wide an audience as possible, while holding his memory dear enough to stave off the advances of Schumann's last protégé, the young Johannes Brahms, whom we'll come to in the section on the Late Romantic composers.

After her husband died, in 1856, Clara continued to tour for more than thirty years. She also found time to be head of piano studies at the conservatoire in Frankfurt, as well as, eventually, caring for a number of her grandchildren and her children (tragically, her son Ludwig ended his days with mental health problems like his father). Her own compositions have become increasingly popular in recent years, a fitting turnaround for someone whose music played second fiddle to that of her husband during her lifetime.

If Paganini was the ultimate violin showman, then **Franz Liszt** (1811–1886) steals the crown in the Romantic piano world. Liszt was also an influential teacher and was tireless in flagging up the work of other composers, particularly Wagner, whom we shall meet later in our story.

Liszt's piano compositions were fiendishly difficult to play – but he wrote them in the knowledge that he would be able to pull off even the seemingly impossible, because of his own brilliant musicianship.

As well as writing his own music, Liszt was adept at turning other people's big tunes into works for the piano. Pieces by Beethoven, Berlioz, Rossini and Schubert were all transcribed by Liszt; he then performed them with his customary style and panache.

Considering that these pieces were originally written for an orchestra, it is remarkable how Liszt manages to make them sound totally complete, even though he had reworked them for just one instrument.

Liszt was undoubtedly a superstar of his day and lived the rock 'n' roll lifestyle a good century or so before it was invented, with a string of sexual liaisons. His decision to take holy orders did nothing to dampen his ardour.

Liszt is also responsible for a change in concerts involving piano and orchestra, which is still in place today. He wanted his adoring fans to be able to see his hands flying up and down the keyboard, so he had the piano turned around. Before then, the pianists used to sit with their backs to the audience.

Charles Gounod (1818–1893) was another keyboard virtuoso, but the organ was his instrument of choice. When he was twenty-one years old, he won the Prix de Rome composition competition and went on to work as an organist in Paris – a pathway followed by many of the great French composers. In his thirties, he began to write operas, but success came only in his forties with *Faust*. He spent a good deal of time in England and his oratorio *Mors et Vita*, one particular part of which has become something of a hit among Classic FM listeners, was premiered at the Birmingham Festival. He is known to many nowadays for his addition to Bach's *Prelude No. 1* of an overlaying tune, which is now usually referred to as 'Gounod's *Ave Maria*'.

Gounod taught our final composer of the Early Romantic period, another Frenchman, **Georges Bizet** (1838–1875). He might be most famous for his opera *Carmen*, but Classic FM listeners are in no doubt as to Bizet's best work. *'Au fond du temple saint'* (known as *'The Pearl Fishers' Duet'*) from his opera *The Pearl Fishers* has consistently been one of the most popular operatic works in the Classic FM Hall of Fame, since we began the chart back in 1996.

Bizet was another of those children who excelled in all things musical at a very young age. He had written his first symphony by the time he was just seventeen. He was also another composer who died tragically young, at the age of thirty-six, probably of throat cancer.

Despite his great talent, poor Bizet never really saw the success that he deserved in his own lifetime. *The Pearl Fishers* had a rocky start, and *Carmen* caused something of a moral outrage among Paris' chattering classes. It really found favour with critics and audiences only in the years after Bizet's death. Since then, it has been performed in the most important opera houses the world over.

Handy Early Romantic Playlist

1   John Field: *Piano Concerto No. 2*
2   Niccolò Paganini: *Violin Concerto No. 2*
3   Carl Maria von Weber: *Clarinet Concerto No. 1*
4   Gioachino Rossini: *'Largo al factotum'* from *The Barber of Seville*

5 Gioachino Rossini: *Overture* from
The Thieving Magpie

6 Gioachino Rossini: *Overture* to *William Tell*

7 Gioachino Rossini: *'Stabat Mater'*

8 Vincenzo Bellini: *'Casta Diva'* from *Norma*

9 Franz Schubert: *'Ave Maria'*

10 Franz Schubert: *Marche Militaire No. 1*

11 Franz Schubert: *Overture* and *Incidental*
Music to *Rosamunde*

12 Franz Schubert: *Piano Quintet in A ('Trout')*

13 Franz Schubert: *Symphony No. 5*

14 Hector Berlioz: *Symphonie fantastique*

15 Hector Berlioz: *The Childhood of Christ*

16 Hector Berlioz: *Requiem*

17 Felix Mendelssohn: *'O for the wings of a dove'*

18 Felix Mendelssohn: *Songs Without Words*

19 Felix Mendelssohn: *Symphony No. 4 ('Italian')*

20 Felix Mendelssohn: *Hebrides Overture*

21 Felix Mendelssohn: *A Midsummer Night's*
Dream

22 Frédéric Chopin: *Nocturne in E flat, Op. 9*
No. 2

23 Frédéric Chopin: *Prelude No. 15 ('Raindrop')*

24 Frédéric Chopin: *Waltz in D flat, Op. 64*
No. 1 ('Minute')

25 Frédéric Chopin: *Piano Concerto No. 1*

26 Robert Schumann: *Kinderszenen (Scenes from Childhood)*

27 Robert Schumann: *'Träumerei' ('Dreaming')*

28 Robert Schumann: *Fantasy in C*

29 Robert Schumann: *Piano Concerto*

30 Franz Liszt: *Hungarian Rhapsody No. 2*

31 Franz Liszt: *Liebestraum No. 3*

32 Franz Liszt: *Piano Concerto No. 2*

33 Franz Liszt: *Rhapsodie espagnole*

34 Charles Gounod: *Judex* from *Mors et Vita*

35 Georges Bizet: *Toreador's Song* from *Carmen*

36 Georges Bizet: *'Au fond du temple saint'* from *The Pearl Fishers*

37 Georges Bizet: *L'Arlésienne Suite No. 1*

38 Georges Bizet: *Jeux d'enfants*

five

The Nationalist Romantics

Here is another of those inexact definitions for you. All of our Romantic composers, and indeed many of our Baroque and Classical composers, could be argued to be 'nationalist' in one way or another.

However, we have grouped together the next thirty-four major composers (all from the Romantic period) because their music is written in a certain style that enables listeners who know a little about their classical music to identify the country of origin.

Sometimes these individual groups are referred to as 'nationalist schools of composers'. This is not a bad description – but think school of dolphins, rather than children sitting in a classroom. A school of dolphins appears to swim together in the same overall direction, although, once you look very closely, you see that each of the animals takes a slightly different route, jumping up, diving down or moving from left to right at different times from their fellow dolphins. It works exactly the same way with schools of composers; although they have common links, they are all writing their own style of music.

The tools composers use to enable listeners to hear the national identity of their music are varied. Sometimes this is achieved through the use of traditional folk songs, tunes and rhythms. On other occasions, composers simply write their own material in the style of their country's traditional music.

The Russian School

If Russian music has a father figure, then **Mikhail Glinka** (1804–1857) is the man. Nationalist composers incorporated the folk music of their native lands into their own music, and Glinka was influenced by the folk tunes that he was introduced to by his grandmother.

Unlike many of the prodigies who litter these pages, Glinka took up music in a serious way only in his late teens and early twenties. His first proper job was as a civil servant in the Ministry of Communications.

When he decided on a change of career, Glinka visited Italy, where he worked as a pianist. It was while he was there that he developed a deep love of opera. When he returned home, he penned his own first opera, *A Life for the Tsar*. Glinka was instantly heralded as the finest Russian composer of the time. His music virtually defined the Russian Nationalist sound overnight. His second opera, *Russlan and Ludmilla*, was nowhere near as successful immediately, although it has stood the test of time better.

He created unquestionably Russian music for the rest of his life, paving the way for a new generation of great Russian composers, all of whom continued to write music that relied heavily on their native folk sounds for its inspiration.

Alexander Borodin (1833–1887) was another composer who had a working life outside music. In fact, he was a much respected scientist. His first published work went under the splendid title *On the Action of Ethyliodide on Hydrobenzamide and Amarien*. You will never hear it played on

Classic FM, though, because it was a scientific paper and nothing to do with music at all.

Borodin was actually the illegitimate son of a Georgian prince. His mother cultivated Borodin's love of music and the arts in general, a passion that he managed to continue to develop throughout his life. He had around only twenty or so works published because he was so busy doing his day job, but these included symphonies, songs and chamber music.

Along with **César Cui** (1835–1918), **Mily Balakirev** (1837–1910), **Modest Mussorgsky** (1839–1881) and **Nikolai Rimsky-Korsakov** (1844–1908), Borodin made up a group of Russians known as 'The Mighty Handful'. Their success was all the more remarkable because all of them actually had jobs away from the world of music – a big difference between them and virtually all the other composers featured in this book.

Borodin is best known now for the *'Polovtsian Dances'* from his only opera, *Prince Igor*. It's worth pointing out that he never completed the opera himself (even though he spent seventeen years working on it), and his friend Rimsky-Korsakov actually finished it off. More about him on page 108.

For our money, Modest Mussorgsky was the most inventive and influential of 'The Mighty Handful', although he shared one or two demons that seem to be very common among highly creative people.

He started out his adult life as an army officer before becoming a civil servant. In his younger days, he was quite a man about town, but he had a fiery temper and struggled with alcoholism throughout his adult life. For this reason, he is often pictured looking dishevelled with an unnaturally bright red nose.

Mussorgsky would often start writing pieces that were never finished. Sometimes, friends would try to help him out by completing them for him, although we can never be quite sure that these pieces actually turned out in the way he initially planned them. Rimsky-Korsakov orchestrated much of Mussorgsky's opera, *Boris Godunov*, and his big hit, *A Night on the Bare Mountain* (which featured in the Disney film *Fantasia*). Mussorgsky's *Pictures at an Exhibition* was orchestrated by Maurice Ravel some years after Mussorgsky originally penned it for piano – and it is this version that is the most popular today.

Despite coming from a wealthy background and having huge talent both as a composer and as a pianist, Mussorgsky died in drink-induced poverty at the age of just forty-two.

Our next composer has already been mentioned as a big musical influence on the lives of both Borodin and Mussorgsky. Nikolai Rimsky-Korsakov was a big player in the development of Russian music, not just as a composer, but also as an orchestrator and teacher (his list of pupils included, among others, Stravinsky, see page 185).

Rimsky-Korsakov's family expected him to go into the navy, and he did not disappoint. They were a little more surprised when he gave up his life on the ocean waves to become a composer and music professor a few years later. In fact, Rimsky-Korsakov had been writing music all along and even started composing his *Symphony No. 1* while at sea, stationed for part of the time off Gravesend in the Thames Estuary. This has to be one of the least glamorous composing locations for any piece of music anywhere in this book.

As well as being remembered for his work sorting out Mussorgsky's music, Rimsky-Korsakov wrote fifteen operas of his own, all of which centred around Russian themes, although he was also influenced by music from further afield. We can particularly hear this in his greatest work, *Scheherazade*, which is based on the story of *The Arabian Nights*. Rimsky-Korsakov had a real skill for writing music that showed off orchestras at their very best. In his work as a music professor, he wrote extensively on the subject, and influenced many of the Russian composers who followed him – most notably Stravinsky.

Pyotr Ilyich Tchaikovsky (1840–1893) took the Russian folk tunes favoured by the Russian nationalist composers, but he did something else with them, infusing them with other influences from across Europe.

Tchaikovsky led a tortured life, principally because of his homosexuality, and he died in mysterious circumstances. He himself said, 'Truly there would be reason to go mad if it were not for music.'

He was a delicate child and throughout adulthood was prone to depression, exhibiting suicidal tendencies on more than one occasion. After studying law, Tchaikovsky was employed briefly as a civil servant before leaving to further his musical studies. He made the mistake of getting married when he was thirty-seven – a relationship that seems to have taken a terrible toll on both him and his wife. She ended up suffering from serious mental health issues, spending her last years in an asylum. For his part, Tchaikovsky became further depressed following the break-up of the relationship just two months after the wedding.

Tchaikovsky was particularly wounded by the poor reception given to his early compositions, and bad reviews also affected his mental state. It is ironic that many of the works involved, such as his *Violin Concerto* and his *Piano Concerto No. 1*, are great favourites today. Indeed, a recording of the *Piano Concerto No. 1* was one of the first classical records to achieve 'gold disc' status, selling millions of copies.

Tchaikovsky wrote ten operas, including *Eugene Onegin*, and ballet scores such as *Nutcracker, The Sleeping Beauty* and *Swan Lake*. Listening to these, nobody can be in any doubt that Tchaikovsky had a massive talent for creating highly melodic, catchy tunes – which is one of the main reasons that his ballets are performed so often today. These great tunes are equally in evidence when you listen to Tchaikovsky's symphonies and piano concertos.

For many years, Tchaikovsky benefited from

the generosity of a rich widow called Nadezhda von Meck, who funded his work on the condition that the two of them should never meet. If ever their paths did cross, they agreed that they would not even acknowledge one another.

It is not entirely clear how Tchaikovsky died. Officially, he was poisoned by drinking water infected by cholera, although there is a school of thought that holds he deliberately took his own life because of fears over being embroiled in a homosexual scandal.

Handy Russian School Playlist

1   Mikhail Glinka: *Russlan and Ludmilla*
2   Mikhail Glinka: *Kamarinskaya*
3   Alexander Borodin: *'Polovtsian Dances'* from *Prince Igor*
4   Alexander Borodin: *In the Steppes of Central Asia*
5   Alexander Borodin: *String Quartet No. 2*
6   Modest Mussorgsky: *A Night on the Bare Mountain*
7   Modest Mussorgsky: *Pictures at an Exhibition*
8   Modest Mussorgsky: *Boris Godunov*
9   Nikolai Rimsky-Korsakov: *Scheherazade*

10 Nikolai Rimsky-Korsakov: *Flight of the
    Bumblebee*

11 Nikolai Rimsky-Korsakov: *Capriccio espagnol*

12 Pyotr Ilyich Tchaikovsky: *Nutcracker*

13 Pyotr Ilyich Tchaikovsky: *1812 Overture*

14 Pyotr Ilyich Tchaikovsky: *Piano Concerto
    No. 1*

15 Pyotr Ilyich Tchaikovsky: *Symphony No. 6
    ('Pathétique')*

16 Pyotr Ilyich Tchaikovsky: *Romeo and Juliet*

17 Pyotr Ilyich Tchaikovsky: *The Sleeping Beauty*

18 Pyotr Ilyich Tchaikovsky: *Swan Lake*

19 Pyotr Ilyich Tchaikovsky: *Violin Concerto*

The Czech School

Czech, Bohemian, Moravian and Slovakian nation-
alism all tends to be clubbed together in this group.
If Glinka is the father of Russian music, then
Bedřich Smetana (1824–1884) occupies the
same role for Czech music. His art and fortunes
were closely tied to his country's struggle for independence, and he manned the barricades during the
failed nationalist uprising in 1848.

He constantly wove Czech stories and places
into his music. There is no better example of

this than his most popular work, *Má Vlast*, which translates as 'My Homeland'. It is a homage to the country of his birth, and took Smetana eight years to complete. Today, the most popular of the work's six sections is *Vltava*, which tells the story of the passage of the River Vltava through Prague.

Smetana ended up suffering from syphilis, deafness and, ultimately, serious mental illness. He was, however, a huge influence on our next composer **Antonín Dvořák** (1841–1904). Dvořák was a Czech and he loved his homeland and its people with the same passion that they adored him.

Dvořák's music was championed by the great Johannes Brahms, who is one of the big players later in this book (see page 143). Gradually Dvořák's fame spread around the world. He had a particularly solid fan base in England with commissions from the Royal Philharmonic Society and the Birmingham and Leeds Festivals.

He then decided to travel to the USA, where he was appointed Director of the National Conservatory of Music in New York in the 1890s. He was terribly homesick for the three years he was in the USA, but he did discover American folk music. He was influenced by these tunes when he was writing his *Symphony No. 9*, which carries the epithet *'From the New World'*. For an entire generation of British television viewers, the slow movement of this magnificent work will forever be known as 'the Hovis music', after its use in a highly memorable television advertising campaign for the bakery.

Dvořák felt the pull of his homeland throughout his time in the USA, and eventually he decided to go back home. He spent his final years working in Prague as a teacher.

Dvořák had one or two other interests outside music: he was an obsessive trainspotter and also developed a strong interest in ships. Indeed, this particular passion might have been one of the reasons he eventually agreed to travel to the USA in the first place, although the enormous riches on offer would have been another strong persuader. He was also something of a pigeon fancier.

When he returned to Prague from the USA, Dvořák mentored a new generation of Czech composers including **Josef Suk** (1874–1935), **Vítězslav Novák** (1870–1949) and **Leoš Janáček** (1854–1928). The last was virtually unknown outside his homeland for most of his life. He worked as a composer, conductor, organist and teacher. His masterpiece is the opera *Jenůfa*, which was first performed when he was fifty years old. It was a success in Brno, where it was premiered, but, because Janáček had fallen out with the head of the Prague Opera, it took another twelve years for the work to reach the Czech capital. When it was finally performed there, the opera was incredibly warmly received, with the result that Janáček, now aged sixty-two, became an overnight success. This spurred him on to compose other acclaimed works, such as *The Cunning Little Vixen* – another opera – and his *Glagolitic Mass*.

Handy Czech School Playlist

1 Bedřich Smetana: *'Vltava'* from *Má Vlast*
2 Bedřich Smetana: *The Bartered Bride*
3 Antonín Dvořák: *Symphony No. 9 ('From the New World')*
4 Antonín Dvořák: *Rusalka*
5 Antonín Dvořák: *Serenade for Strings*
6 Antonín Dvořák: *Slavonic Dances*
7 Antonín Dvořák: *Cello Concerto*
8 Leoš Janáček: *Sinfonietta*

The Scandinavian School

In Norway and Finland **Edvard Grieg** (1843–1907) and **Jean Sibelius** (1865–1957) were both musical firebrands in their countries' respective nationalist movements. Under the influence of the Norwegian violinist and folk historian **Ole Bull** (1810–1880), Grieg composed a huge body of music, particularly for the piano, in the national style.

Grieg was another of those composers who had a passionate love affair with the country of their birth. And his fellow Norwegians loved him just as much as he loved them. It could so easily have been very different, though. Grieg was actually of Scottish descent: his great-grandfather emigrated from Scotland to Scandinavia after the Battle of Culloden.

As a youngster, Grieg showed great flair for the piano and he was sent to Leipzig to study music. Despite not particularly enjoying himself there, Grieg honed his musical genius in the city.

Grieg was best suited to writing small-scale works, such as his *Lyric Pieces* for solo piano, but his most famous concert work is his beautiful *Piano Concerto*, which includes a very dramatic opening with notes pouring from the piano over the top of a drum roll.

Grieg is buried halfway up the side of a rock face, near Troldhaugen. Apparently, the composer was out walking one evening and noticed how the sun hit a spot, halfway up the mountainside. He told a friend who was with him, 'There . . . I would like to rest for ever!'

Sibelius's music is infused with Finnish folk mythology. His greatest work, *Finlandia*, is seen by Finnish people as being musically representative of their homeland, in the same way that the English tend to see many of Elgar's works as embodying their national characteristics. Sibelius was, like Mahler, also regarded as a master of the symphony.

Alongside the piano, Sibelius's first love was the violin. He longed to be a concert violinist, although he also studied composition from books, and gradually this became the dominant focus in his musical life. When he was twenty-seven, he composed *En Saga*, a tone poem, and *Kullervo*, a nationalist choral symphony. Seven years later he wrote his *Finlandia*.

The composition of *Finlandia* also coincided, more or less, with Sibelius's first foray into symphonies, which, from then on, were to form the backbone of his musical output. He consoled the violinist inside himself by writing a *Violin Concerto* when he was thirty-eight. He wrote his *Symphony No. 5* during the First World War and by 1924, he had completed seven symphonies.

Away from music, Sibelius was a heavy drinker and smoker, and he suffered from throat cancer in his forties. He was also hopeless with money and was given a state pension so that he could continue composing without having to worry about his finances. More than twenty years before his death, Sibelius stopped composing any music at all. He lived out the rest of his days in a fairly solitary state. He had particularly strong views on those who were paid to comment on his work: 'Pay no attention to what the critics say. No statue has ever been put up to a critic.'

Handy Scandinavian School Playlist

1   Edvard Grieg: *Piano Concerto*
2   Edvard Grieg: *Holberg Suite*
3   Edvard Grieg: *Peer Gynt Suite No. 1* (includes *Morning* and *In the Hall of the Mountain King*)
4   Jean Sibelius: *Karelia Suite*
5   Jean Sibelius: *The Swan of Tuonela*

6   Jean Sibelius: *Finlandia*

7   Jean Sibelius: *Valse triste*

8   Jean Sibelius: *Violin Concerto*

9   Jean Sibelius: *Symphony No. 5*

The Spanish School

Although classical music was being written in Spain in the nineteenth century, the country was by no means a hotbed of famous composers. One exception is **Isaac Albéniz** (1860–1909), who was a bit of a tearaway as a youngster.

It's said that Albéniz could play the piano at just one year old. Three years later he was performing in public, and by the age of eight he was on the road plying his musical trade.

Albéniz was truly brilliant at improvising and could make up and vary tunes on the piano without a moment's thought. He often performed party pieces on the piano for money. He would stand with the keyboard behind him, and would play tunes with the backs of his hands. It is an incredibly difficult stunt to pull off. And, just for good measure, Albéniz used to do it dressed up as a musketeer, of all things. He had plenty of adventures as a youngster and by the time he was fifteen he had already performed in countries as far afield as Argentina, Cuba, the USA and England.

As an adult, Albéniz led a far more conventional existence and became particularly famed for his very Spanish-sounding solo piano work, *Iberia*. His success brought Spanish music out of the shadows and to the attention of international audiences.

Albéniz was a big influence on many other composers from the Spanish nationalist school, including **Enrique Granados** (1867–1916), **Manuel de Falla** (1876–1946) and **Heitor Villa-Lobos** (1887–1959), who was actually Brazilian.

After studying in Paris and Barcelona, Granados went on to found his own concert season and piano school in the Spanish city. In his day, he was a pianist first and a composer second. He was especially highly regarded as a performer of his own piano works. His music is unquestionably Spanish in style and this has ensured his enduring popularity in his homeland. Granados and his wife were both drowned when the *Sussex*, the boat they were travelling on from Liverpool to Dieppe, was torpedoed by a German submarine. Classical music was robbed of a talent who would have continued on to even greater things.

Manuel de Falla spent his twenties studying piano and composition and started to receive recognition for his music only when he had almost turned thirty. He moved to Paris in 1907 and became friends with the French composers Debussy, Ravel and Dukas. He also met the Russian composer Stravinsky and the great ballet impresario Diaghilev. After the First World War, he went back to Spain. Diaghilev commissioned de Falla to write the score for the ballet *The Three-Cornered Hat*, which had its premiere at the Alhambra Theatre in London's Leicester Square, next door to where Classic FM's studios are based today. Becoming disillusioned with his homeland because of the Spanish Civil War, he spent the last seven years of his life in Argentina.

Although we have included him in the Spanish school, a reminder here that Villa-Lobos was actually born in Rio de Janeiro. He studied music with his father until he was twelve years old, at which point he became a guitarist in a Brazilian street band – something he would later commemorate in his *Chôros*. From the age of sixteen onwards, he made money playing the cello in a theatre orchestra, but also began to study his country's folk music.

He was funded by the government to study in Paris, returning as a music educator and composer when he was forty-three; he founded the Brazilian Academy of Music. For the last two decades of his life, he benefited from the championship of the conductor Leopold Stokowski, who was instrumental in bringing his music to a wider audience. Today his most enduring works outside his home country are his *Bachianas brasileiras,* a fusion of Bach and Brazil.

Handy Spanish School Playlist

1   Isaac Albéniz: *Suite española*
2   Isaac Albéniz: *Iberia*
3   Enrique Granados: *Spanish Dance No. 5*
4   Manuel de Falla: *The Ritual Fire Dance* from the ballet *El amor brujo*
5   Heitor Villa-Lobos: *Bachianas brasileiras*

The English School

It's been a while since we have been in England. In fact **Arthur Sullivan** (1842–1900) is the first English composer we have featured in the Romantic period. The Germans were not slow in noticing England's failure to deliver the goods for well over a century. They took to referring to England as 'the land without music'.

Arthur Sullivan is still famous today. However, history has been rather unfair to him because he is best known for what might not actually have been his best work. In the 1870s, Sullivan began a partnership with the librettist W. S. Gilbert. They collaborated on a series of light-hearted operettas, including: *Trial by Jury, The Pirates of Penzance, HMS Pinafore, Princess Ida, The Mikado* and *The Yeomen of the Guard*.

The Mikado gave the Gilbert and Sullivan partnership its longest run during their lifetimes, with 672 performances. It ran in London and New York and eventually transferred to Vienna and Berlin, where hits such as *'A Wand'ring Minstrel, I'* and *'Three Little Maids from School Are We'* were greeted with rave reviews, before the show moved on to France, Holland, Spain, Belgium, Germany and Russia.

Despite their enormous success, the two men never really saw eye to eye and had a series of extremely heated rows. One of their most spectacular bust-ups was about a new carpet at the Savoy Theatre in London, where their operettas were usually staged.

Sullivan was desperate to be treated as a serious composer, but by and large his non-operetta works are now forgotten. He wrote an opera, *Ivanhoe*, and an attractive *Symphony in E*. He also wrote the tune to the hymn *'Onward! Christian Soldiers'*, which probably now counts as his most performed work.

Sir **Charles Hubert Hastings Parry** (1848–1918) was very much a man of his age. After Eton and Oxford (he completed his music degree at the age of eighteen while still at Eton), he became an underwriter at Lloyd's of London. Following seven years in the City, studying music in his spare time, he gave up business for composition – earning extra money writing articles for the august *Grove Dictionary of Music and Musicians*, the first volume of which was published in 1878.

Parry taught successfully for many years, his star pupils including Vaughan Williams and Holst. His own compositions rapidly put him at the head of the musical establishment and his large-scale choral works, notably *'I Was Glad'* and *'Blest Pair of Sirens'* are still staples of the repertoire. He is probably best known, however, for his *Jerusalem*. In 1916, he set Blake's visionary poem to music for 'Fight for the Right', a women's suffrage movement.

Some years later, Elgar reorchestrated the piece and it is this version that is still sung at the Last Night of the Proms in the Royal Albert Hall every year. When he heard it, King George V is said to have remarked that he wished it could take the place of the National Anthem.

Although he is now somewhat forgotten, it is a mark of the esteem in which Sir **Charles Villiers Stanford** (1852–1924) was held in his day that he was buried in Westminster Abbey, next to Henry Purcell. He was born in Dublin and was educated there and at Queens' College, Cambridge, where, at his father's insistence, he read classics rather than music. Nevertheless, it was his time at Cambridge – he conducted the Music Society orchestra and became organist at Trinity College while still an undergraduate – that put him firmly on the musical map.

After further study in Germany, Stanford began composing in earnest. His prodigious musical output includes seven symphonies, ten operas, fifteen concertos, chamber, piano and organ pieces, songs and more than thirty large-scale choral works. However, it was his role as Composition Professor at the then new Royal College of Music that enabled him to leave a real mark on musical posterity.

The Scottish composer **Hamish MacCunn**
(1868–1916) was a pupil of both Hubert Parry
and Charles Villiers Stanford at the Royal College
of Music, hence his inclusion here in the English
school. Something of a 'one-hit wonder', MacCunn
was born in Greenock. When his studies were over,
he went on to take a teaching post when he was
barely out of his teens. He tasted success early with
his concert overture *The Land of the Mountain and
the Flood* when he was just twenty-one years old.

From then on, he never quite composed anything to rival it in the public's affections, but that
did not stop him from working and he was much
in demand as an opera conductor. He conducted
the Carl Rosa Opera Company and later frequently
stood in for Sir Thomas Beecham. He was a particularly ardent advocate of Scottish music. In his
forties, he was appointed Head of Composition at
the Guildhall School of Music. Gradually, his health
deteriorated, not helped by his heavy workload of
conducting, composing and teaching and he died
when he was just forty-eight years old.

Our final composer in the English school could
possibly claim the title of being the least prolific in
the whole of this book, due to his hugely self-critical

nature and to his life being tragically cut short in the First World War. The entire output of **George Butterworth** (1885–1916) numbers just eleven works, almost all of which were composed in the four years just before he joined the army. Had he lived, he would surely have been destined for greatness. He was an avid collector of folk songs, through which he became friendly with Ralph Vaughan Williams, whom we will come to in a few pages' time. Rather more surprisingly he was also an enthusiastic folk dancer. He was awarded the Military Cross after his death in the trenches on the Somme. Vaughan Williams dedicated his *London Symphony* to his memory.

Handy English School Playlist

1 Arthur Sullivan: *HMS Pinafore*
2 Arthur Sullivan: *The Mikado*
3 Arthur Sullivan: *Ivanhoe*
4 Arthur Sullivan: *Symphony in E*
5 Hubert Parry: *'I was Glad'*
6 Hubert Parry: *Jerusalem*
7 Charles Villiers Stanford: *Magnificat in G*
8 Hamish MacCunn: *The Land of the Mountain and the Flood*

The French School

France's answer to Gilbert and Sullivan's English operettas came in the form of works by **Jacques Offenbach** (1819–1880), a man who obviously had a sense of humour. He was born in the town of Cologne and would sometimes sign himself as 'O. de Cologne'.

Offenbach also unleashed the can-can on an unsuspecting French public in 1858. The can-can comes from the operetta *Orpheus in the Underworld*, which scandalised the chattering classes of Paris at the time of its premiere. (You might have noticed by now that talkative types in the French capital seemed rather to enjoy being in a permanent state of shock and outrage at the artistic extravagances of one French composer or another.)

If you think the title of Offenbach's operetta sounds familiar, then you would be right. It is the same story that Peri, Monteverdi, Purcell and Gluck all set to music in previous centuries. Offenbach's version was very satirical, much more fun than the previous incarnations, and was riotously debauched in places. Despite the initial shock, it proved to be very successful and Offenbach never really looked back.

The other work for which he is most remembered is the more serious opera *The Tales of Hoffmann*, which features the *Barcarolle*.

By no means as influential as Offenbach, **Léo Delibes** (1836–1891) is remembered now chiefly for his opera *Lakmé*, which includes *The Flower Duet*. This was used to great effect in a long-running British Airways advertising campaign. Delibes also wrote two notable ballets, *Coppélia* and *Sylvia*.

Delibes was not without influential friends – he worked for both Berlioz and Bizet when he was chorus master at Paris's Théâtre Lyrique.

Among the leading opera composers in France in the latter part of the nineteenth century, **Jules Massenet** (1842–1912) was a child prodigy taught first by his mother and then – you've guessed it – at the Paris Conservatoire. He made his recital debut at the age of sixteen and from then on paid his way by giving music lessons and by performing in cafés, bars and orchestras.

When he was twenty-one, he won the Prix de Rome, the major French composition prize. He served alongside Georges Bizet in the army during the Franco-Prussian War, before going on to make a name for himself with his operas. His major successes came in the 1880s, first with *Manon* and later with *Le Cid*. There followed a relatively unsuccessful period, even though it saw the premiere of *Werther*, now considered to be one of Massenet's greatest successes. Everything changed with *Thaïs*, which proved to be an enduring hit, not least because of its beautiful *Méditation* – which is a popular party piece for many violin soloists.

Other composers in the French nationalist school include **Emmanuel Chabrier** (1841–1894), **Joseph Canteloube** (1879–1957) and **Charles-Marie Widor** (1844–1937). Living to a ripe old age meant that while Widor's early memories might well have been of the Revolution of 1848, he was still around to witness Franklin D. Roosevelt's second term in office, more than ninety years later. The son of an organ builder, he studied with his father and later in Brussels before landing one of the most prestigious posts in France – organist at St Sulpice, Paris.

Later, as organ and then composition professor at the Paris Conservatoire, Widor devoted his efforts to furthering the cause of the organ in music. His greatest legacy is his body of ten symphonies for the solo organ, in which he put the instrument through its paces, keen to show that it was capable of emulating the whole orchestra.

Finally, one of Belgium's greatest classical music exports, who sneaks into the French school by dint of his training. **César Franck** (1822–1890) was touring by the age of eleven and moved with his family to Paris to study at the Conservatoire there. Until relatively late on during his life, his music failed to capture the imagination of the French public. He worked as an organist and rose to fame for his playing – and particularly for his improvisations. At the age of fifty, he became a professor at the Conservatoire. Gradually, his works were performed more and more. His pleasant demeanour and general good nature led to him being nicknamed 'Père Franck' by those who knew him.

Handy French School Playlist

1 Jacques Offenbach: *The Tales of Hoffmann*
2 Jacques Offenbach: *Orpheus in the Underworld*
3 Léo Delibes: *Lakmé*
4 Léo Delibes: *Coppélia*
5 Léo Delibes: *Sylvia*
6 Jules Massenet: *Méditation* from *Thaïs*

7   Charles-Marie Widor: *Toccata* from *Organ
     Symphony No. 5*
8   César Franck: *Panis angelicus*

The Viennese Waltz School

Our next two composers from among the Nationalist
Romantics might well be father and son, but the
time lag between the two generations was not great,
with just twenty-one years separating the two men's
birthdays. **Johann Strauss Snr** (1804–1849) is
known as 'the Father of the Waltz'. He was a fine
violinist and set up an orchestra when he was just
twenty-two that toured all over Europe, with great
financial success. Strauss was eventually booked at
the Sperl Ballroom in Vienna, where he became
famous, also playing regularly for the court balls.
Despite composing a couple of hundred waltzes,
he would eventually be eclipsed by his son, and
remembered, pretty much, for one work: the
Radetzky March.

Johann Strauss Snr might have been 'the Father
of the Waltz', but it was **Johann Strauss Jnr**
(1825–1899) who was to earn the title 'the Waltz
King'. His father didn't want him to take up the
violin, but the younger Strauss did so anyway, at the

age of nineteen, going on to set up a new orchestra to rival that of his dad. Strauss Jnr had a keen business brain and soon he was earning serious riches.

In the process, Strauss Jnr wrote nearly 400 waltzes, including the most popular of them all, *By the Beautiful Blue Danube*. In the end, he had six Strauss orchestras running simultaneously, two of which were conducted by his brothers Josef and Eduard (each of whom had around 300 compositions to his name). Spotting the potential of the stage, he switched to operetta when he was fifty-six; his greatest example being *Die Fledermaus (The Bat)*, which has become a staple of the operatic repertoire.

Strauss Jnr's waltzes and polkas were an instant hit in the coffee houses of Vienna, and their light, jaunty style proved to be popular all over Europe. Classical music enthusiasts who take themselves too seriously sometimes consider the Strauss family's oeuvre to be beneath them. Don't let them influence you! This family knew how to write a great tune that can lift your spirits and reverberate around your head for days after you first hear it. It's a concept that the wildly successful violinist and orchestral leader André Rieu has caught on to almost a century and a half after the Strausses were at their peak. Rieu has become a multi-million-selling recording artist through his championing of the music of Johann Strauss Jnr and his contemporaries.

The brothers of Johann Strauss Jnr – Josef and Eduard – were by no means the leading lights of the Strauss family, but they did perform an important role in keeping the tradition going. Josef deputised as conductor of the band and had a hand in the composition of the *Pizzicato Polka* with his elder brother Johann. Eduard took over the band in 1872, and brought it to the UK. A polka specialist rather than a waltz king, he is also the brother responsible for burning all the original manuscripts of the entire Strauss clan, which is why today we have some works only in piano versions.

Our final member of the Viennese school was completely unrelated to the Strauss family – although he was both a contemporary and a rival. **Franz von Suppé** (1819–1895) was born in the then Dalmatian city of Spoleto (now Split in Croatia). His musical talent was spotted by the local bandmaster and choirmaster. When he moved to Vienna, aged sixteen, he was determined to study music, despite false starts in law and medicine.

He soon became not only an opera conductor, but also a singer, composing a huge number of stage works along the way and becoming a serious rival to Johann Strauss Snr for the title of the Viennese Offenbach. However, the overtures to his operettas *Poet and Peasant* and *Morning, Noon and Night in Vienna* fare better these days than do the operas themselves.

Handy Viennese Waltz School Playlist

1 Johann Strauss Snr: *Radetzky March*
2 Johann Strauss Snr: *By the Beautiful Blue Danube*
3 Johann Strauss Snr: *Die Fledermaus*
4 Johann Strauss Snr: *Tales from the Vienna Woods*
5 Johann Strauss Snr: *Tritsch-Tratsch Polka*
6 Johann Strauss Snr: *Thunder and Lightning Polka*
7 Franz von Suppé: *Overture* to *Light Cavalry*
8 Franz von Suppé: *Overture* to *Poet and Peasant*
9 Franz von Suppé: *Overture* to *Morning, Noon and Night in Vienna*

six

The Late Romantics

Many of our final group of Romantic composers were still writing music well into the twentieth century, but they appear in this chapter rather than the next because they still have that Romantic sound to their work.

It is worth noting that many of these Romantic composers had strong friendships with some of the other composers discussed in the previous two chapters.

It also bears saying once again that there was so much great music being composed at the same time in different countries around Europe that any attempt to group the composers together in this way will be, to a certain extent, completely subjective. Although most reference books are very

clear on which composers belong in the Baroque
and Classical eras, things start to become a little
fuzzier around the edges when it comes to the end
of the Romantic period and the beginning of the
twentieth century.

We begin with one of the lesser-known composers of the period. **Henry Litolff** (1818–1891) was
one of those people who was always destined to
have an event-filled life. His mother was Scottish
and his father was a dance-master prisoner-of-war
from the Alsace region of France. After studying
music, Litolff eloped to Gretna Green to get married at the age of seventeen. He separated from
his wife and ended up in prison, before escaping
with the assistance of the jailer's daughter. He was
finally divorced and then married again, before getting divorced for a second time and married for a
third time. His third wife died and – at the age
of fifty-five – he married once again, this time to
a seventeen-year-old. Amazingly, he also found the
time to compose music and is chiefly noted for the
Scherzo from his *Concerto sinfonique No. 4.*

In nineteenth-century Italy, one opera composer stood head and shoulders above all others:
Giuseppe Verdi (1813–1901). He had a big bushy

moustache and beard, and photographs show him with a glint in his eye.

Born near Busseto in Parma, Verdi showed musical promise very early; by the time he was seven, he was already helping the organist at the local church. Though he was turned down for a place at the Milan Conservatoire because of his youth, he persuaded Vincenzo Lavigra, a Milanese composer, to give him private composition lessons.

Verdi's operas are packed full of great tunes. In total, he wrote twenty-six operas, most of which are still being performed today. They include many of the best-known operatic arias of all time.

Verdi was a big hit with opera audiences across Italy, and when *Aida* received its premicre, the standing ovation at the end was so prolonged that the company made no fewer than thirty-two curtain calls.

Nonetheless, there was sadness in Verdi's life, too. He outlived both of his wives and two of his children. His music generated considerable wealth and when he died he left his riches to a retirement home for musicians, which he had had built in Milan. He said that he regarded this as a greater work than all of his music.

Although he is best known for his operas, no discussion of Verdi's life would be complete without mention of his *Requiem*. It is regarded as one of the greatest pieces of choral music of all time. Although it was always intended to be a purely choral work, it is full of drama and rather operatic in style.

Our next composer was not a nice man. In fact, he was the most odious character with the most hateful views in the whole of this book. If we were choosing composers to include in this book in terms of their personalities, then **Richard Wagner** (1813–1883) simply would not make it. However, we are judging the music – not the man – and so no history of classical music is complete without his inclusion.

Wagner's brilliance as a composer is not in doubt. Some of the most important and impressive music of the whole of the Romantic period came from his pen, especially in the world of opera. Yet he was an anti-Semitic racist, a serial philanderer, who was prepared to lie, cheat and steal to get what he wanted, and he would ride rough-shod over people, casting them aside without further thought. Wagner had a monstrous ego, a vile temper, was wildly eccentric and appeared almost to believe that he was some form of deity.

It is for his operas that Wagner is chiefly remembered. He took German opera to a whole new level and, although he was born in the same year as Verdi, the sound he created was very different from that of the Italian operas of the same period. He called what he wrote 'the music of the future'.

One of Wagner's big ideas was to give each of his main characters a musical theme that recurred in the music at the points when they were at the forefront of the action. (This is one of the first significant uses of a leitmotif, recurring musical mottos associated with a particular character, place or even an idea.) It might seem very logical to anyone who is a fan of musicals today, but at the time it was a revolutionary idea.

Wagner's greatest triumph was the *Ring* cycle, which is made up of four operas: *Das Rheingold*, *Die Walküre*, *Siegfried* and *Götterdämmerung*. These tend to be performed over four consecutive nights and last well in excess of fifteen hours. These four operas represent a huge achievement for one man, and just because we find his views so objectionable, that should not take away from their magnificence.

Length is something of a trademark for Wagner.

His final opera, *Parsifal*, is well over four hours long. The conductor David Randolph described it as 'the kind of opera that starts at six o'clock and after it has been going three hours you look at your watch and it says 6:20'.

Wagner completed *Parsifal* in 1882, by which time he was seriously ill with angina. He died of a heart attack while recuperating in Venice, and was buried in the grounds of his Bayreuth villa.

The life of composer **Anton Bruckner** (1824– 1896) is a lesson in never giving up. He was a hard worker, thinking nothing of practising for twelve hours a day in his job as an organist. He taught himself much of what he knew about music and graduated from a correspondence course on composition at the ripe old age of thirty-seven.

An organist by trade, Bruckner is most respected today for his symphonies – he wrote eleven of them in total although they are only numbered up to nine. He gave his *Symphony in D minor* the title *'Die Nullte'*, which means that it tends to be catalogued as *No. 0*. Bizarrely, before he got going with his *Symphony No. 1 in C minor*, he wrote a further *Symphony in F minor*, which often appears in lists of his works as *Symphony No. 00*.

He was sometimes racked with self-doubt, but he did at least achieve acclamation, although much later in life than he deserved. The critics finally told him they loved him following the premiere of his *Symphony No. 7*. He was sixty years old.

Johannes Brahms (1833–1897) was not one of those composers born with a silver baton in his hands. Instead, he came from a relatively poor background, or at least from a good family who were no longer as rich as they had been. As a teenager, Brahms would earn money by playing the piano in brothels around his native Hamburg. It's fair to say that he had already seen something of the seedier side of life by the time he was an adult.

Brahms' music was championed by Robert Schumann, and the two men became friends. When Schumann died, Brahms grew closer to Clara Schumann, eventually falling passionately in love with her. It's not clear exactly how close they became, although Brahms' relationship with her might have coloured his judgement of other women, because nobody else seems to have held the same significance in his affections.

Brahms was quite a curt and short-tempered man, but his friends claimed that he had a softer

side, which he did not always show towards stran-
gers. On his way out of a party, he once said, 'If
there is anyone here whom I have not insulted, I
beg his pardon.'

Brahms would not have won any prizes in a
'best turned-out composer' competition. He hated
to buy new clothes and often wore baggy trousers
that were covered in patches and nearly always
too short. On one occasion, his trousers nearly fell
down altogether in the middle of a performance.
Another time, he was forced to take off his tie and
use it as a belt to keep his trousers from ending up
around his ankles.

Brahms' musical style owes much to the influences of Haydn, Mozart and Beethoven, and some
music experts believe him to be a composer who
still wrote in the style of the Classical period some
years later than was strictly fashionable. That said,
Brahms did introduce some new ideas. He was particularly adept at developing small groups of notes
in his music and stretching them out throughout
the piece – what musicians call a 'recurring motif'.

Brahms was not an opera man, but otherwise
wrote excellent examples of just about every other
genre of classical music. This has, quite rightly,

meant that he is regarded as one of the giants among the composers in the whole of this chapter. His own view on his music was to the point: 'It is not hard to compose, but it is wonderfully hard to let the superfluous notes fall under the table.'

In his last decade, Brahms composed the masterly *Quintet in B minor for clarinet and strings* but by the time Clara Schumann died in 1896, he was already physically deteriorating. He died a year later.

Born just five years after Brahms, **Max Bruch** (1838–1920) would have been completely eclipsed by his fellow German had it not been for one piece of music – his *Violin Concerto No. 1* which he composed when he was twenty-eight years old. Arguably, he spent the rest of his life trying to emulate that success. Bruch himself recognised this fact when he said, with a modesty that is rare among composers, 'Fifty years from now, Brahms will loom up as one of the supremely great composers of all time, while I will be remembered for having written my G minor Violin Concerto.'

How right he was. But what a piece to be remembered for! Bruch did compose many other works – around 200 in all – especially a number of big choral pieces and some operas, which tend not to be performed that often today. His music is big on tunes, but he did nothing really to break new ground. In fact, he was not that keen on the music of his fellow composers who were trying to innovate.

Noted for his somewhat grumpy personality, Bruch spent a few bad-tempered years as Principal Conductor of the Liverpool Philharmonic Orchestra from 1880, but three years later he was on a boat to a new job in the USA. The orchestra's players were not great fans. But during his time on Merseyside, he did produce *Kol Nidrei*, a soulful setting for cello and orchestra of a Jewish prayer; it is considered to be one of his best works. He was also briefly in charge of the Scottish Orchestra (now the Royal Scottish National Orchestra) between 1898 and 1900.

We have already come across a galaxy of prodigious stars, but French composer **Camille Saint-Saëns** (1835–1921) arguably tops the lot. When he was just two years old, Saint-Saëns could already play tunes on the piano – and he had mastered reading and writing, too. A year later, he started to pick out his own compositions on the piano. Just four years after that, he had added a mastery of lepidopterology to his talents (that's the study of butterflies and moths). By the time he was ten, Saint-Saëns had no problem at all in playing piano works by Mozart and Beethoven. His other areas of expertise included geology, astronomy and philosophy. There was no getting away from it – he was a clever kid. He entered the Paris Conservatoire where his dazzling talents won him the admiration of Gounod, Rossini, Berlioz and Liszt.

After studying at the Paris Conservatoire, Saint-Saëns worked as an organist for many years, starting off in a small church on the rue Saint-Martin, before moving in 1857 to the prestigious La Madeleine, where he remained until 1875. As he got older, he became more influential in French musical life, and ensured that the music of composers such as J. S. Bach, Mozart, Handel and Gluck all received regular performances.

Composing was always Saint-Saëns' first love. As well as his symphonies he turned out symphonic poems, concertos, chamber music, church music and thirteen operas, though only one of these, *Samson and Delilah*, is much performed today.

Saint-Saëns' best-known work is *Carnival of the Animals*, which he banned from public performance during his lifetime. He was worried that he would not be taken seriously as a composer once the critics heard it. It's great fun, with the orchestra depicting a lion, hens and cocks, tortoises, an elephant, kangaroos, an aquarium, a jackass, a cuckoo, birds, pianists, fossils and a swan.

Some of Saint-Saëns' other music was written for less-often-heard combinations of instruments, including his famous *Symphony No. 3 ('Organ')*, which was used in the film *Babe*.

In old age, Saint-Saëns found himself falling out of musical favour. Although he had started off as a radical composer, he hated the music of his younger contemporaries. He spent much of his time travelling, passing his last years in Algiers, where he died from pneumonia in 1921. He is buried in the Montparnasse Cemetery in Paris, along with other great composers including Emmanuel Chabrier, Georges Auric and César Franck.

Saint-Saëns was an influence on other French composers, including **Gabriel Fauré** (1845–1924). The younger man took over from Saint-Saëns as organist of the Church of La Madeleine in Paris.

Although Fauré's talent was nowhere near as prodigious as his mentor's, he was also a fine pianist. He was not a wealthy man, and needed his job as organist, choirmaster and teacher to pay the bills. That meant relegating composition to his spare time but, despite this, he clocked up well over 250 published works. Some of these were a long time in their gestation: Fauré's *Requiem* took more than twenty years to write.

In 1905, Fauré was made director of the Paris Conservatoire and was accorded the status necessary for him to have a big say in the development of French music at the time. He retired fifteen years later and struggled with his hearing late in life.

Today, Fauré is well respected outside France, although his music remains far more popular there than elsewhere.

For fans of English music, the arrival of **Edward Elgar** (1857–1934) must have been something of a relief. Many musical historians regard him as the first really significant English-born composer since Henry Purcell way back in the Baroque period, although we did stop off at Arthur Sullivan on our journey through classical music history, not to mention acquiring George Frideric Handel along the way.

Elgar loved England dearly, particularly his native Worcestershire, where he spent most of his life, taking the beautiful countryside of the Malvern Hills as his inspiration.

His childhood was steeped in music: his father ran the local music shop in Worcester and was the organist at the local church. The young Elgar was taught the instrument by his father and by the time he was twelve years old, he was already the reserve organist at church services.

After a year working in a solicitor's office, Elgar decided to try to make his way in the far less financially secure world of music. He worked as a jobbing musician for a while, giving violin and piano lessons, playing the violin in local orchestras, and even doing a little conducting.

Gradually, Elgar's reputation as a composer grew, although it was a hard slog for him to break through into the public consciousness outside the area in which he lived. By the turn of the twentieth century, Elgar was composing extensively, fulfilling a particular need from English festivals and music societies for big choral works. He already had *The Black Knight*, *King Olaf* and *The Light of Life* under his belt, although he was still teaching the violin to pay the bills. It was his *Variations on an Original Theme* that did the trick. This work is now better known as the *Enigma Variations*. First performed in London in 1899, this piece has fostered more debate than almost any other British classical music work. It is dedicated to a group of Elgar's friends, each of whom is represented by the musical characteristics in each of the fourteen individual movements. There was, however, added mystery. Elgar suggested that there was an 'enigma' hidden in the piece, possibly a second well-known tune. Nobody has ever satisfactorily unlocked the code, although many people have spent a lot of time trying. Elgar took the secret of the enigma to his grave.

Elgar was knighted in 1904 and became Master of the King's Music in 1924. His music is now seen as being intensely English, and his work is often called into play at major national events. His *Cello Concerto* has a sense of the English countryside about it; *'Nimrod'* from the *Enigma Variations* is often played at times of national remembrance; and his *Pomp and Circumstance March No. 1* is more commonly known as *'Land of Hope and Glory'*.

Elgar was a private man who loved family life. He did, however, leave behind one other magnum opus – his big, bushy moustache. For many years it was a feature of the Bank of England's £20 notes.

Apparently, the detail of his whiskers made the notes particularly hard for counterfeiters to copy.

New York-born **Edward MacDowell** (1860–1908) spent twelve years living in France and Germany from the age of sixteen. He studied first at the Paris Conservatoire and then with the Swiss composer Joachim Raff. His composing career really began to take off once his music was championed by Liszt. He returned to his homeland and was hailed as the new hero of American classical music. His *Piano Concerto* went down particularly well and he was appointed the first ever Professor of Music at Columbia University in New York. He struggled to balance the demands of university life with those of being a composer and eventually gave up the day job. Not long afterwards, he suffered a mental breakdown from which he never recovered. One little-known fact about MacDowell: he wrote his first few pieces under the pseudonym 'Edgar Thorn'.

Back in Italy, **Giacomo Puccini** (1858–1924) was the natural heir to Giuseppe Verdi at the top of the Italian opera composers' league.

Puccini's family had always been involved in church music, but after he saw a performance of

Verdi's *Aida*, Puccini found the call of the opera too great to ignore.

After studying in Milan, Puccini's first big operatic success was *Manon Lescaut* in 1893. After that, he had success after success after success: *La bohème* in 1896, *Tosca* in 1900 and *Madam Butterfly* in 1904.

In all, Puccini composed twelve operas, with *Turandot* his final one. He died with just a small part of the work still unwritten. This was completed by another composer, but at its premiere, the conductor Arturo Toscanini stopped the orchestra playing exactly at the point where Puccini stopped composing. He turned to the audience and said, 'Here, death triumphed over art.'

With Puccini's death and the premiere of *Turandot*, the Italian operatic composing tradition was also snuffed out. There are no more great Italian opera composers to come in our history of classical music. Who knows if the tradition will be rekindled again with a new, as yet undiscovered, talent in the future?

Pietro Mascagni (1863–1945) was a fellow student of Puccini at the Milan Conservatoire. His father was an Italian baker who had set his heart on his son becoming a lawyer. However, after an uncle fixed up some music lessons for the youngster, he proved to be so good that a journey towards a conservatory education became inevitable.

Mascagni's first big job was as a conductor with a touring opera company. Next, he turned his hand to composition, concentrating on complicated, innovative modern music. He changed tack for his one-act opera *Cavalleria rusticana,* which his wife entered into a competition. It won, beating seventy-two other compositions. At this stage, Mascagni was still only twenty-five years old. It was produced in Rome in 1890, before being performed around the globe – at one point, *Cavalleria rusticana* was being staged in ninety-six different opera houses around the world simultaneously. It made him a fortune and although he never wrote anything else to match it, he was still reasonably successful as a composer and a conductor.

Another of those great Italian *verismo* composers, **Ruggero Leoncavallo** (1857–1919) was born in the same year as Edward Elgar into a well-off family (his father was a police magistrate). Leoncavallo studied at the Naples Conservatoire. There was little interest in his early output either as a composer or a librettist and he ended up working as a café pianist in places as far apart as Paris, London and Egypt.

Leoncavallo was hugely influenced by the operas of Wagner and set out to try to emulate his success. In 1890, though, he heard Mascagni's *Cavalleria rusticana*, which is as unlike Wagner as anything can be imagined. Leoncavallo composed his opera *Pagliacci* shortly afterwards. Today, it is often performed in tandem with *Cavalleria rusticana* in a double-bill (known as *'Cav & Pag'* in the trade).

Leoncavallo, though, was not as fortunate with his version of *La bohème*. It was first performed just over a year after Puccini's immortal opera of the same name was premiered and there was only ever likely to be one winner.

During his lifetime **Gustav Mahler** (1860–1911) was famous as a conductor rather than a composer. He tended to do the former during the winter and the latter during the summer.

Mahler was the second of fourteen children and his father owned a distillery in Bohemia. The story goes that, as a boy, Mahler discovered a piano in his grandmother's attic. Just four years later, at the age of ten, he gave his first public performance.

Mahler studied at the Vienna Conservatoire, where he began composing. In 1897, he became conductor of the Vienna State Opera, a job he would hold with great success for the next ten years.

Mahler himself began to write three operas, although he never finished any of them. Today, we think of him as one of the great composers of symphonies. He is responsible for one of the big blockbusters of the genre, his *Symphony No. 8*, which has more than 1,000 musicians joining together in one way or another: as part of the orchestra, the enormous choir or as solo singers.

After his death, Mahler's music was out of fashion for nearly fifty years before it was revived in Britain and the USA in the second half of the twentieth century.

Born in Germany, **Richard Strauss** (1864–1949) was not part of the Viennese Strauss dynasty (see pages 132–4). Although he lived for almost the first half of the twentieth century, he is still regarded as one of the great German Romantics. His international standing fell when he decided to continue working in Germany after 1939, although he was acquitted of being a Nazi collaborator at the end of the Second World War.

Strauss was a fine conductor, which allowed him to develop an intimate understanding of just how orchestras worked. He put this insight into practice throughout his career as a composer. He was also keen to pass on his experience to other conductors, saying, 'Never look at the trombones, it only encourages them' and 'Don't perspire while conducting, only the audience should get warm'.

Strauss is best remembered today for the opening to *Also Sprach Zarathustra*, which was used in the Stanley Kubrick film *2001: A Space Odyssey*, but he wrote some fine operas – among the best to come from Germany ever – including *Der Rosenkavalier*, *Salome* and *Ariadne auf Naxos*. He also composed the very beautiful *Four Last Songs* for voice and orchestra just a year before he died. They were not actually the last songs that Strauss wrote, but they serve as a fitting finale to his composing career.

Another German of the time, **Max Reger** (1873–1916) is among the very few composers with a palindrome for a surname. The Bavarian-born Reger was a virtuoso organist, as well as a composer, and his performances did much to rekindle popularity for the instrument. He also had a passion for the music of Bach and Beethoven. Having settled in Munich at the age of twenty-eight, Reger won fame as a solo performer and an accompanist, before moving to take up the post of Director of Music at the University of Leipzig. A heavy drinker, he died from a heart attack, aged only forty-three. He is remembered for his mordant wit as well as for his music. He famously responded to a critic, 'I am sitting in the smallest room of my house. I have your review in front of me. Very shortly it will be behind me.'

Born in Moscow, **Alexander Scriabin** (1872–1915) was the son of a lawyer and a pianist. Unsurprisingly, he excelled in piano from a young age, and despite being enrolled at a military cadet school in early boyhood, managed to keep up his playing. When he was sixteen, he switched to studying music at the Moscow Conservatoire, tackling composition with the composer Arensky as well as continuing his piano studies. A publishing deal he made while still at college allowed him to tour his own works when he was just twenty-four.

Scriabin became piano professor at his old conservatoire aged twenty-six, but gave it up to settle in Switzerland in 1903. He was increasingly attracted to theosophy and other mystical philosophies, composing his works from this time onwards as heralds, so he said, of forthcoming disaster. He also had the condition synaesthesia – taking the form in his case of 'seeing' musical pitches in colour. Accordingly, he designed what he called a *clavier à lumières* – a 'colour organ' – to feature in his massive symphonic work *Poem of Fire*. Instead of sounds, it projected colours when played.

Our final Late Romantic composer is another man who lived until the middle of the twentieth century, and he actually composed many of his biggest hits in the 1900s. Yet he is still considered to be a Romantic composer – in fact, for our money, he was the most Romantic of the lot.

Sergei Rachmaninov (1873–1943) was born in Semyonovo, near Novgorod in north-western Russia, into a family that was not as well off as it had once been. As a child, his musical talents were recognised and he was sent off to study, first in St Petersburg and then in Moscow.

Rachmaninov was a stunningly good pianist, and developed as a fine composer, writing his *Piano Concerto No. 1* when he was just nineteen. He also found time to pen his first opera, *Aleko*.

Rachmaninov was never the happiest soul, and

many photographs show him looking decidedly grumpy in front of the camera. It was something that his fellow Russian composer, Igor Stravinsky, noticed: 'Rachmaninov's immortalising totality was his scowl. He was a six-and-a-half-foot-tall scowl ... he was an awesome man.'

When Rachmaninov played for Tchaikovsky, the older man was so impressed that he gave him an 'A++++' on his score sheet – the highest marks ever given in the Moscow Conservatoire's history. Rachmaninov quickly became the talk of the town.

Nevertheless, things were not to go so well for Rachmaninov for too long. When his *Symphony No. 1* was premiered, it received a terrible panning from the critics and Rachmaninov sank into a deep depression. His work rate slowed considerably, and he started to have trouble composing anything at all.

In the end, Rachmaninov went to see a hypnotherapist called Dr Nikolai Dahl, who managed to set him back on the road to recovery. And, by 1901, Rachmaninov finished the piano concerto that he had been trying so hard to write for ages. He dedicated his work to Dr Dahl, and it was regarded as a triumph by Russian audiences. The new work was his *Piano Concerto No. 2*, which has been a favourite of classical music lovers across the world ever since. Indeed, when we combined together all of the votes from the first sixteen years of our annual Classic FM Hall of Fame listeners' poll, we found that this piece of music was the winner at the top of the chart, by quite some margin.

Rachmaninov began to tour across Europe and to the USA. When he was in Russia, he continued working as a conductor and composer. Following the Russian Revolution in 1917, Rachmaninov took his family off on a tour of Scandinavia. He never went back home. Instead, he moved to Switzerland, where he had a house on the banks of Lake Lucerne. He had always loved rivers and boats and was, by now, a rich man.

Rachmaninov was a brilliant conductor and he had this advice for those who also wanted to excel in this field: 'A good conductor ought to be a good chauffeur. The qualities that make the one also make the other. They are concentration, an incessant control of attention, and presence of mind – the conductor only has to add a little sense of music.'

In 1935, Rachmaninov decided that he would make even more of a fortune by returning to the

USA. First he lived in New York, before finally moving to Los Angeles. Once he was there, he set about building himself a new home that was absolutely identical to the one he had left behind in Moscow.

As he grew older, Rachmaninov conducted less and less – and composed hardly at all. It was as a pianist that he reached the height of his fame.

Despite missing his homeland, Rachmaninov enjoyed everything that the USA had to offer. He was incredibly proud of his large Cadillac, and often offered to drive guests home from his house, just so that he could show it off.

Just before he died, Rachmaninov became an American citizen. He was buried not in Russia, but in his new homeland, in New York.

The End of the Romantic Period

Across three chapters, we have dedicated more pages to the Romantic period than to any other era of classical music. And for good reason – there was so much music being written in so many different places that the musical commentators of the time must have had trouble keeping up. There was a real change in the sound of classical music during this period, with the most popular composers ending up writing music with big, rich, lush orchestral sounds. In many ways, Rachmaninov best exemplifies this. When you think back to a composer such as Beethoven, who was still writing music at the start of the Romantic period, it's easy to see just how much things have changed.

However, if you think the sound of classical music changed during the eighty or so years of the Romantic period, then that is nothing to what happened afterwards. Over the next hundred or so years – taking us right up to the present day – things really start to sound very different indeed.

Handy Late Romantic Playlist

1   Henry Litolff: *Scherzo* from *Concerto Sinfonique No. 4*

2   Giuseppe Verdi: *'Celeste Aida'* from *Aida*

3   Giuseppe Verdi: *The Grand March* from *Aida*

4   Giuseppe Verdi: *Overture* to *La forza del destino*

5   Giuseppe Verdi: *'Questa o quella'* from *Rigoletto*

6   Giuseppe Verdi: *'La donna è mobile'* from *Rigoletto*

7 Giuseppe Verdi: *Drinking Song* from
La traviata

8 Giuseppe Verdi: *Anvil Chorus* from
Il trovatore

9 Giuseppe Verdi: *Chorus of the Hebrew Slaves*
from *Nabucco*

10 Giuseppe Verdi: *'Dies Irae'* from *Requiem*

11 Richard Wagner: *Overture* from *The Flying
Dutchman*

12 Richard Wagner: *Prelude* to Act 3 of
Lohengrin

13 Richard Wagner: *Bridal Chorus* from
Lohengrin

14 Richard Wagner: *Ride of the Valkyries* from
The Valkyrie

15 Richard Wagner: *Siegfried's Funeral March*
from *The Twilight of the Gods*

16 Richard Wagner: *Pilgrims' Chorus* from
Tannhäuser

17 Richard Wagner: *Prelude* to *Tristan and Isolde*

18 Anton Bruckner: *Symphony No. 7*

19 Anton Bruckner: *Symphony No. 8*

20 Anton Bruckner: *'Locus Iste'*

21 Johannes Brahms: *Academic Festival Overture*

22 Johannes Brahms: *Hungarian Dance No. 5*

23 Johannes Brahms: *Piano Concerto No. 1*

24 Johannes Brahms: *Symphony No. 4*

25 Johannes Brahms: *Violin Concerto*

26 Max Bruch: *Violin Concerto No. 1*

27 Max Bruch: *Scottish Fantasy*

28 Max Bruch: *Kol Nidrei*

29 Max Bruch: *Symphony No. 3*

30 Camille Saint-Saëns: *Carnival of the Animals*

31 Camille Saint-Saëns: *Danse macabre*

32 Camille Saint-Saëns: *Violin Sonata No. 1*

33 Camille Saint-Saëns: *Symphony No. 3* ('Organ')

34 Gabriel Fauré: *Requiem*

35 Gabriel Fauré: *Cantique de Jean Racine*

36 Gabriel Fauré: *Dolly Suite*

37 Gabriel Fauré: Incidental music to *Pelléas et Mélisande*

38 Edward Elgar: *Enigma Variations*

39 Edward Elgar: *Cello Concerto*

40 Edward Elgar: *Chanson de matin*

41 Edward Elgar: *Pomp and Circumstance March No. 1*

42 Edward Elgar: *Salut d'amour*

43 Edward Elgar: *Serenade for Strings*

44 Edward MacDowell: *To a Wild Rose*

45 Giacomo Puccini: *'Che gelida manina'* from *La bohème*

46 Giacomo Puccini: *'O soave fanciulla'* from *La bohème*

47 Giacomo Puccini: *'O mio babbino caro'* from *Gianni Schicchi*

48 Giacomo Puccini: *'Un bel di'* from *Madam Butterfly*

49 Giacomo Puccini: *The Humming Chorus* from *Madam Butterfly*

50 Giacomo Puccini: *'Nessun dorma'* from *Turandot*

51 Giacomo Puccini: *'Vissi d'arte'* from *Tosca*

52 Pietro Mascagni: *Intermezzo* from *Cavalleria rusticana*

53 Ruggiero Leoncavallo: *'Vesti la giubba'* from *Pagliacci*

54 Gustav Mahler: *Symphony No. 1 ('Titan')*

55 Gustav Mahler: *Symphony No. 2 ('Resurrection')*

56 Gustav Mahler: *Symphony No. 5*

57 Gustav Mahler: *Symphony No. 8 ('Symphony of a Thousand')*

58 Richard Strauss: *Also Sprach Zarathustra*

59 Richard Strauss: *Four Last Songs*

60 Max Reger: *Cello Suite No. 1*

61 Alexander Scriabin: *Etude in D sharp minor,*
    Op. 8 No. 12

62 Sergei Rachmaninov: *Piano Concerto No. 2*

63 Sergei Rachmaninov: *Piano Concerto No. 3*

64 Sergei Rachmaninov: *Rhapsody on a Theme of*
    Paganini

65 Sergei Rachmaninov: *Symphony No. 2*

66 Sergei Rachmaninov: *Vocalise*

seven

The 20th Century

Modern or Contemporary?

We are back to that issue of trying to label classical music again, and its stubborn resistance to being categorised into a series of boxes. The composers that we cover in this chapter were all writing music in the twentieth century, and many books would consider them to be 'modern' or 'contemporary' composers. However, we're not quite sure that this label is appropriate any more.

Consequently, we have divided the next two chapters into the twentieth century and the twenty-first century, with those composers who have been writing music since the year 2000 in the second category.

For this reason, we are not convinced that we should refer to composers who have been dead for more than seventy or eighty years as being 'contemporary' or 'modern'. Maybe somebody will come up with a better title for these composers one day, but in the meantime we are gathering them under the heading 'The Twentieth Century'.

What Else Was Going On in the World?

This was the century when the world became the place that we know now. Telephones, radios, television, widespread car ownership, international air travel, space exploration, home computers, compact discs, the Internet – all of these developments changed the way in which people lived their lives.

Two world wars had a huge impact on society and international relations. This century also saw a change in the world order, with the USA and Russia taking on superpower status.

The Innovators

Our first twentieth-century composer, **Claude Debussy** (1862–1918) was an innovator through and through. He was responsible for changing all sorts of rules about how classical music should be written. Debussy lived in Paris, which was going through a phase of being at the very centre of classical music development during his lifetime.

While he was studying, Debussy showed a precocious talent for composing music with harmonies that were completely out of the ordinary. He is seen as an 'Impressionist' composer, and spent much of his time with the painters who were grouped together under the same heading.

Debussy took the inspiration for his music from paintings, works of literature and from the artists who lived near his flat in the Montmartre district of Paris. He was particularly fascinated with all things oriental.

Debussy had a complicated private life, with two of his lovers attempting to shoot themselves when he began relationships with new women. Ultimately, he fought a long battle with cancer. By the time he finally succumbed to the disease, Debussy had achieved widespread international fame.

Debussy's music was so different that when you listen to it and compare it with what had come before, it is easy to understand why he is seen as something of a torch-bearer for those composers who followed.

Another Frenchman, **Erik Satie** (1866–1925) took individualism in his music to the absolute extreme.

Born in Honfleur, Satie spent his early years being shunted between there and Paris, where his parents had moved when he was six years old. After an unsuccessful spell at the Paris Conservatoire – 'a local penitentiary', as he put it – he became a cabaret pianist at Montmartre's famous 'Chat Noir'.

It would be fair to say that Satie was an odd man, and this was reflected in the titles that he gave to some of his works: *Veritable Flabby Preludes (for a Dog)*; *Sketches and Exasperations of a Big Boob Made of Wood*; *Five Grins or Mona Lisa's Moustache*; *Menus for Childish Purposes*; *Three Pear-Shaped Pieces* (there were seven of these); *Waltz of the Chocolate Almonds*; and *Things Seen from the Right and Left without Spectacles*.

One of Satie's strangest compositions is called *Vexations*. It is made up of the same few bars of music, which are played over and over again a total of 840 times. Unsurprisingly, this has never been a big concert hall hit, although every so often it is given an outing – usually more as a publicity stunt than a serious concert performance.

Satie's idiosyncrasies are also apparent in his ballet, *Parade*, which was created for Diaghilev with the story provided by Jean Cocteau, and features parts for typewriter, whistle and siren. All this madness aside, he did write some beautiful solo piano works, including his famous *Gymnopédies*, although his sister Olga, who knew him as well as anyone, should probably have the last word on Erik: 'My brother was always difficult to understand. He doesn't seem to have been quite normal.'

He died, from cirrhosis of the liver, brought about through years of heavy drinking, in 1925.

We stay in France for our third composer of the twentieth century. **Maurice Ravel** (1875–1937) achieved unimaginable fame thanks to the decision by Jayne Torvill and Christopher Dean to choose his *Boléro* as their musical accompaniment as they skated their way to an Olympic gold medal and into the British sporting hall of fame in 1984. Almost three decades later, both the music and the skaters were given a new lease of life on the prime-time ITV1 programme *Dancing on Ice*.

Another 'Impressionist' composer, Ravel was

often clubbed together with Debussy. He was also a musical innovator and, again like Debussy, he did not always see eye to eye with the French musical Establishment. He tried three times to win the Prix de Rome, the most prestigious prize offered by the Paris Conservatoire. His lack of success acquired the status of a scandal; his music was considered too radical by the conservatives who judged the competition.

He produced a succession of great works, such as the opera *L'heure espagnole*; *Valses nobles et sentimentales*, which he composed for the piano but later rescored for orchestra; and the ballet *Daphnis et Chloé*, which he wrote for Diaghilev's Ballets Russes. It was through this commission that Ravel met Stravinsky, who became a firm friend, although his relationship with Debussy deteriorated over time.

A brilliant pianist, Ravel composed widely for the instrument, but for many people *Daphnis et Chloé* is his greatest work, despite the famous *Boléro* threatening to eclipse it in the public's mind. Though it is possibly his best-known composition, Ravel himself came to dislike the latter work, describing it as 'a piece for orchestra without music'.

Ravel was a short man and was not allowed to fight in the First World War. Instead, he worked as an ambulance driver and was deeply affected by the scenes of carnage that he witnessed. The sadness he felt is mirrored in the music he wrote at the time, such as the very moving *Le tombeau de Couperin*.

Leaving France behind, we travel back across the Channel to England, to a man who must rank alongside Edward Elgar as the most English of composers.

Ralph Vaughan Williams (1872–1958) was born in the very quaint-sounding Gloucestershire village of Down Ampney. A pronunciation note before we get started: Vaughan Williams' first name rhymes with the word 'safe'.

Vaughan Williams began collecting traditional English folk songs from a young age. He used these tunes later in life as the central plank of many of his great successes. He studied at the Royal College of Music in London, at the same time as Gustav Holst. The two became lifelong friends.

Following some time spent studying with Ravel in Paris, Vaughan Williams returned to England to write *On Wenlock Edge* and incidental music to *The Wasps* (for a Cambridge student production). This was also the time of successes such as *Fantasia on a Theme of Thomas Tallis* and *A London Symphony*. In total he wrote nine symphonies, six operas and a ballet, as well as numerous hymn tunes and scores for stage and screen. His music has deservedly seen a steady rise in popularity over the last twenty years, with *The Lark Ascending*, which is written for violin and orchestra, proving to be particularly popular among Classic FM listeners, regularly topping our annual Hall of Fame poll of listeners' classical music tastes. This piece is similar to many of his other works in the way in which it manages to paint a picture of the English countryside.

By the way, Ralph Vaughan Williams was not the only famous name in his family – his great-uncle was Charles Darwin and on his mother's side he was directly descended from the pottery magnate Josiah Wedgwood.

Another Gloucestershire boy, **Gustav Holst** (1874–1934) was born in Cheltenham, where his father was an organist and piano teacher. Holst was of Swedish descent, and his full name was Gustavus von Holst. He became concerned during the First World War that he might be mistaken for being German, so he shortened his name.

A trombonist by trade, Holst turned out to be a very gifted teacher and, for many years, he was director of music at St Paul's School for Girls in London. He drew on English folk tunes for the inspiration for many of his works, although he was also inspired by subjects as far apart as astrology and the poetry of Thomas Hardy. Asked about his composing, Holst said, 'Never compose anything unless not composing it becomes a positive nuisance to you.'

It is easy to think of him as a 'one-hit wonder' today because of the enormous success of *The Planets*. Six of the seven movements represent the astrological influences of the planets: Mars (war), Venus (peace), Jupiter (jollity), Uranus (magic), Saturn (old age) and Neptune (mysticism). Mercury, the winged messenger of the gods, is the star of the other movement. You will notice that Pluto is not included in this list. The reason is simple – it had not yet been discovered at the time that Holst composed the work. (Composer Colin Matthews has plugged this gap and his *'Pluto'* is now sometimes played alongside Holst's suite.) Although *The Planets* is often performed as a complete work, *'Jupiter'* has a life all of its own as the tune to the great English rugby hymn *'I Vow to Thee My Country'*.

The third of our quartet of twentieth-century English composers is Bradford's most famous son, **Frederick Delius** (1862–1934). His father was a prosperous wool merchant who didn't like the idea of his boy following a career in music. In an attempt to distract him from composing, Delius was sent to run an orange plantation in the USA. This actually had the opposite effect and inspired Delius to write *Appalachia*, which relies on African-American spirituals as its core.

While he was in the USA, Delius took lessons from an American organist, Thomas F. Ward. When he returned to Europe, Delius's father gave up fighting his son's musical aspirations and the young man was sent to study in Leipzig.

After that, Delius moved to Paris, where he spent much of the rest of his life. He specialised in 'idylls' for orchestra, as well as choral works and operas. Thanks in the main to the advocacy of the conductor Sir Thomas Beecham, who became the composer's lifelong champion and friend, it is the 'idylls' that have endured the best – wonderful meanderings of orchestral colour, rich in fleeting melodies. They are also exquisitely crafted.

While he was in Paris, he contracted syphilis,

the symptoms of which made his life particularly unpleasant some thirty years later. He relied on a young Yorkshireman, Eric Fenby, to transcribe his final works.

Much of Delius's music is as English as it is possible for a piece of music to be. Take *Brigg Fair: An English Rhapsody*, for example. This set of variations is based on a folk song that hails from Lincolnshire.

One of England's most underrated composers, **Gerald Finzi** (1901–1956) deserves to be mentioned in the same breath as Elgar and Vaughan Williams. His settings of the poems of Thomas Hardy are particularly beautiful. He did a lot to revive the music of older and lesser-known English composers, such as William Boyce and John Stanley, with performances of their works being given by his group, the Newbury String Players. Two interesting footnotes: between 1941 and 1945, he worked in the Ministry of War Transport; he also became an expert cultivator of rare apples.

An amazing child prodigy, **Fritz Kreisler** (1875–1962) entered the Vienna Conservatoire at the age of seven. He won the first prize at the Paris Conservatoire when he was still only twelve years old and was on tour by the time he was fourteen. He then turned his back on a career in music, opting instead to study medicine at university and then to become an officer in the Austrian army.

He took up the violin again at the age of twenty-four and resumed his international performing career. In 1910, he gave the first performance of Elgar's *Violin Concerto* – the work is dedicated to him. He had to lay down his violin again to fight in the Austrian army in 1914, but was discharged after being wounded at the front. He was one of the first darlings of the gramophone age and his archive recordings can still be heard today. He claimed that many of the violin pieces he composed to show off his own virtuosic playing were written by composers from the 1700s, when in fact they were all his own work.

Australian-born composer **Percy Grainger** (1882–1961) challenges Erik Satie for the title of 'most eccentric composer' in our book. He married his 'Nordic Princess' Ella Viola Ström in front of thousands at the Hollywood Bowl. He was nicknamed 'the Jogging Pianist' because he used to run to piano concerts and rush up on stage at the last minute. Not only did he make his own clothes, but he also designed the early prototypes of the women's sports bra. A good friend of Grieg and Delius, he was a great collector of folk tunes. He spent the latter part of his life inventing complicated musical formats using early electronic instruments.

Our next composer is somebody about whom it's impossible not to have a view. Some people would say he should not appear in this book; others would say he is one of the greatest composers of the twentieth century. Few people who have heard his music have no opinion at all. **Arnold Schoenberg** (1874–1951) never really made it as a wildly popular composer among ordinary concert-goers, but he was very influential and widely admired by other composers.

At first, Schoenberg wrote pieces in the Romantic style, but then he developed a totally different way of composing, with a wholly new set of rules. Previously, composers had written music in various keys or sets of keys, with guidelines governing areas such as harmony and melody. These guidelines also had the effect of maintaining a gentleman's distance from dissonant or discordant music. Schoenberg threw these rules out of the window, in favour of a strict regime whereby no one note could be repeated until all other eleven had been played. (There are twelve pitches available in the chromatic scale – think of all the black and white notes on a piano between two notes of the same name.) This equality between all twelve notes – called twelve-tone music, or serialism – often resulted in music that could sound jarring or discordant.

We play very little of Schoenberg's music on Classic FM because our listeners tell us that they don't like it. However, we have included him in this book because he was without doubt an incredibly important figure in twentieth-century classical music, although the music he wrote is definitely an acquired taste.

It's important to stress that although other composers were influenced by Schoenberg, by no means all of them wrote music like he did.

So far, we have featured only one other great Hungarian composer in detail in this book – the marvellous piano virtuoso Franz Liszt. But **Béla Bartók** (1881–1945) wrote music that was far more Hungarian-sounding than his predecessor's. In fact, Hungarian folk music became the abiding passion of Bartók's life.

Together with his great friend and fellow composer **Zoltán Kodály** (1882–1967), Bartók criss-crossed the country, gathering recordings of authentic Hungarian tunes on a primitive machine, which imprinted the sounds on wax cylinders. The two men kept careful records of everything they heard, producing one of the finest recorded archives of any country's music. Before this, tunes were passed from person to person and were not written down anywhere. As no recordings had previously been made, many of these tunes would have died out completely had it not been for the efforts of Bartók and Kodály.

Bartók became a music professor in Budapest, but he decided to leave the country with the onset of the Second World War. He took up a job at an American university, where he composed and gave piano concerts. Once there, he was not the hit he had been in his homeland and, in 1945, he died of leukaemia. Bartók left behind one particularly interesting work, his *Concerto for Orchestra*. Usually concertos are for a solo instrument and an orchestra, but Bartók believed that the Boston Symphony Orchestra, for whom it was written, was so great that it deserved to have a concerto composed for solo groupings from within the orchestra.

Kodály was the son of a music-loving employee of the state railway company and his first orchestral piece was played by his school orchestra while he was still a pupil. Much later in life he became an important figure in the Hungarian music scene, occupying some of the most prestigious academic music jobs in the country. Towards the end of his life he was still travelling extensively around Europe and the USA conducting his own works.

Another of Hungary's musical greats, **Franz Lehár** (1870–1948) studied at the Prague Conservatoire, but learned much from his father, who was a military bandmaster. Despite being told by Dvořák to spend as much time as he possibly could composing, he took up roles as an orchestral violin player and worked in his father's band, as well as taking on a variety of different conducting jobs.

Lehár got his break as an operetta composer somewhat fortuitously. When the librettists of *The Merry Widow* were casting around to find a composer to set their lyrics to music, his name was suggested, though in fact he was only their second choice. He got the job by playing a song over the telephone. The operetta initially received a somewhat mixed reception, nearly closing before it had properly opened, but eventually Lehár found that he had a hit on his hands.

Born in St Petersburg, Russia's **Alexander Glazunov** (1865–1936) had lessons from Rimsky-Korsakov, who said that he progressed 'not by the day, but literally by the hour'. He was lucky enough to find a rich sponsor in Mitrofan Belyayev early on, so a lot of his music was published and paid for without any of the struggles that other composers had to endure. Belyayev introduced him to Liszt, who became an influence on the young composer. Glazunov's music is on the conservative side, but that does not mean that it is not beautiful – his *Saxophone Concerto* of 1931 is particularly stunning. As an instrumentalist, he was something of a polymath, learning to play the piano, violin, cello, trumpet, French horn, clarinet and a range of percussion instruments.

Igor Stravinsky (1882–1971) was a giant among twentieth-century composers. He was always keen to innovate and was often at the forefront of new trends in the way that classical music was written.

Stravinsky was lucky enough to have Nikolai Rimsky-Korsakov as his teacher when he was a boy.

He never received any other formal instruction in how to compose.

As an adult, Stravinsky's talents were spotted by the great ballet impresario, Sergei Diaghilev. He had the power to make or break composers. Diaghilev commissioned Stravinsky to write *The Firebird*, which was based on an old Russian folk story. It was a big hit.

Stravinsky's next commission for Diaghilev was *Petrushka* – another ballet and another massive critical and box office success. Things didn't go so well when the two men paired up once again though. Stravinsky's *Rite of Spring* performed by Diaghilev's Ballets Russes with choreography by Vaslav Nijinsky and designs by Nicholas Roerich, caused mayhem at its premiere, with a riot breaking out in the audience. This was not just the odd murmuring of discontent, but full-on fighting. Half the audience was outraged by what it heard and the other half recognised Stravinsky's talent for innovation and was prepared to defend the work.

Stravinsky moved from Russia to Switzerland, and then to France, and finally to the USA, where he set up home, first in Hollywood and then in New York. He had never been afraid to reinvent himself musically, and his writing changed in style considerably over the years. At times he was particularly radical and during other periods he was more conformist to the classical music norms. These chameleon-like qualities extended to Stravinsky's life away from music as well. Along the way, he managed to change his nationality three times.

Stravinsky was always ready with a witty one-liner, whether talking about other composers, his audiences or just classical music in general. You will find him quoted in other places in this book, but here are two of his sayings that remain personal favourites: 'Too many pieces of music finish too long after the end' and 'To listen is an effort, and just to hear is no merit. A duck hears also!'

Another giant of twentieth-century Russian music, **Sergei Prokofiev** (1891–1953) was one of the many composing whizz-kids whom we have encountered in this book. In his case, he had managed to clock up two whole operas by the time he was eleven. After studying at St Petersburg Conservatoire, where he made a name for himself as a very challenging modernist composer, Prokofiev continued to write music that, to be frank, shocked his audiences. Like Stravinsky, he too was commissioned to write two ballet scores by Diaghilev, but neither enjoyed the great success of Stravinsky's big hits.

Prokofiev decided to move to the USA after Lenin took control in Russia, and he achieved major success as a concert pianist. He was commissioned to turn his piano work *The Love for Three Oranges* into an opera. It had a rocky beginning, but has eventually become one of his best-loved pieces – and certainly his most successful opera.

In 1936, Prokofiev decided to return home to Russia, but his timing was terrible as his arrival coincided with the period in which the state started to dictate what composers could and could not write. At first, he managed to co-exist with the Soviet authorities. His *Violin Concerto No. 2* went down well, as did his *Symphony No. 5*. However, his next symphony got him into the Communist Party's bad books. At one stage, Prokofiev faced charges of composing music that worked against the state, but he battled through.

Aside from his work for the concert hall, Prokofiev became widely respected for his magnificent ballets. *Romeo and Juliet* is the best known of them, though the Bolshoi, for whom he originally wrote it, declared it impossible to dance. He also composed some striking film scores, notably for Eisenstein's epics – *Alexander Nevsky* and *Ivan the Terrible* – as well as a mammoth opera, *War and Peace*.

It seems a rather cruel irony that Prokofiev died of a brain haemorrhage on the same day that Stalin – the man who had done so much to oppress his music over the years – also died.

Rimsky-Korsakov's influence as a teacher of other great composers did not just extend as far as the borders of Russia. Talented musicians travelled from far and wide to learn from him. One such was the Italian **Ottorino Respighi** (1879–1936). He studied first in his home town of Bologna, becoming a proficient violinist, before taking lessons in composition in Russia with Rimsky-Korsakov and, briefly, in Berlin with Bruch. As well as playing in a string quartet, he became the Director of the Academy of St Cecilia in Rome before giving up the position to allow himself more time to compose. He is best remembered today for his orchestral 'pictures' – studies such as the *Fountains of Rome* and the *Pines of Rome*, as well as *The Birds*, which replicates authentic bird calls. Respighi was much admired by Mussolini, though he claimed not to reciprocate the Italian dictator's feelings.

Another Italian, Venice-born **Ermanno Wolf-Ferrari** (1876–1948) divided his time as a boy between music and art, choosing first to follow in the footsteps of his artist father and study painting at Rome's Accademia di Belle Arti. He switched to music, having moved to Munich when he was seventeen years old, studying for a time with the composer and librettist Arrigo Boito.

Seemingly, Wolf-Ferrari was more appreciated in Germany than in Italy, certainly during his lifetime. He spent the First World War years in Switzerland, composing little – a silence he broke only when he was in his forties. When he was sixty-three, he was made Professor of Composition at the prestigious Mozarteum in Salzburg. He died in his native Venice, aged seventy-two.

Aram Khachaturian (1903–1978) is the only Armenian composer in our book. He studied in Moscow, incredibly, managing to win a place at the Gnessin Music Academy to study the cello, even though he had never played the instrument before. He built up his reputation with works such as his *Piano Concerto* and *Violin Concerto*, as well as the ballets *Gayaneh* and *Spartacus*, the latter being his best-known piece. Prokofiev was a fan and Khachaturian held a selection of government-sponsored posts, until he wrote some music that earned the disapproval of the state, at which point he moved to writing film scores. He is seen today as having been the foremost proponent of Armenian folk music.

You might have seen this man's name on the side of pharmaceutical products because **Francis Jean Marcel Poulenc's** (1899–1963) father was a wealthy chemist who owned the family firm Rhône-Poulenc.

Poulenc was the most famous of a group of French composers who were known as 'Les Six'. (The others were Louis Durey, Darius Milhaud, Germaine Tailleferre, Arthur Honegger and Georges Auric).

Poulenc became well known for his ballet *Les biches*, and then for a long series of popular French songs. His composing style changed, though, following the death of a friend. He became more religious and his music reflected his newly found faith. This period saw him write a number of religious works, including his magnificent *'Gloria'*.

Poulenc is also known to generations of children as the composer of *The Story of Babar, the Little Elephant*. It remains as good a way as any of introducing youngsters to classical music.

Jean Françaix (1912–1997) was a gifted pianist, performing with Poulenc on more than one occasion. He had music in his blood – his mother was a singing teacher and his father was the Director of the Le Mans Conservatoire. Ravel was a big influence on the young Françaix, as was his teacher Nadia Boulanger, who also guided the American composers Aaron Copland, Leonard Bernstein and Philip Glass. After winning first prize for piano at the Paris Conservatoire, Françaix travelled extensively around Europe and the USA, giving concerts wherever he went. He didn't let the performing get in the way of his work as a composer, though, writing more than 200 separate pieces during his long life. His best loved today is *L'horloge de flore* ('The Flower Clock'), a work for oboe and orchestra that focuses on a group of flowers, each of which blooms at a different time of day. The movement celebrating the *Malabar Jasmine* – a particular Classic FM favourite – comes into flower at three o'clock in the afternoon.

Our next quartet of pre-war composers were all from the USA. American classical music had been quietly developing its influence on the world stage and this foursome did an enormous amount to burnish the country's musical credentials.

John Philip Sousa (1854–1932) was born in Washington DC to a family of Portuguese descent. From singing and violin-playing during his childhood, Sousa moved via theatre orchestras to directing first the Marine Band and then his own group of musicians. From the age of thirty-eight, he toured his band with amazing success across the USA, Europe and much of the rest of the world; indeed, wherever you are in the UK, you are never very far from a former Sousa concert date.

Sousa composed more than 130 marches, becoming known as 'The March King' and creating his own marching bass brass instrument, the Sousaphone, in the process. He wrote his *'Stars and Stripes Forever'* on Christmas Day in 1896, and played it at pretty much every concert he gave for the next thirty-six years of his life. By the time he died in 1932, it had become the USA's national march.

Our next trio of pre-war composers were all

from the USA. Although we have mentioned America many times so far – particularly during the Romantic period – we have not yet featured any American composers.

Probably the biggest earner of all classical composers in his own lifetime, **George Gershwin** (1898–1937) was banking as much as US$250,000 a year, which was no mean feat in the 1930s. He wrote a succession of very successful Broadway shows, film scores and orchestral works. A virtuoso pianist himself, he toured the USA and Europe.

With a background in writing hit musicals, Gershwin knew a good tune when he heard one, and his orchestral works, such as *Rhapsody in Blue* and *An American in Paris*, have show-stoppingly tuneful moments. His opera *Porgy and Bess* includes songs such as *'Summertime'* and *'I Got Plenty o' Nuttin''*, which are still performed with great regularity today.

They say that opposites attract and one of Gershwin's fans was none other than Arnold Schoenberg. It is hard to think of two men who wrote more contrasting music. In fact, the two played tennis together.

Gershwin died at the tragically young age of thirty-eight from a brain tumour. He continued to take lessons on writing for orchestra well into his thirties and it seems certain that, had he lived, he could well have gone on to become an even greater success as a classical composer. His music remains hugely popular on both sides of the Atlantic today, not least because the knack of being able to pen an infectiously catchy tune never left him.

Our next composer holds the distinction of being the only one so far to have lived entirely in the twentieth century. The son of New York Jewish immigrant parents, **Aaron Copland** (1900–1990) was a musically talented teenager who decided he could learn more by studying in Paris. By the time he returned to New York, he had an idea that he wanted to develop a truly American sound to his music. Although it was without doubt classical music that he wrote, Copland managed to blend in elements of jazz and folk music.

Copland wrote a series of blockbuster ballet scores including *Billy the Kid*, *Rodeo* and *Appalachian Spring* – all of which are now regarded as being as American as apple pie. His *Fanfare for the Common Man* features at the inauguration of the President of the United States of America. Not bad for a guy whose parents were from Russia.

After the Second World War, Copland changed his writing style and started to adopt the 'serialism' advocated by Schoenberg. The pieces he wrote in this period of his life were nowhere near as popular as those that had come before, although he did once say, 'Composers tend to assume that everyone loves music. Surprisingly enough, everyone doesn't.'

Samuel Barber (1910–1981) composed music that was Romantic in style, long after the Romantic period had disappeared. In fact, he was born in the year when we consider the Romantic period to have ended altogether.

Barber was not an innovator like Schoenberg, Stravinsky or Copland, and he certainly didn't write big showy tunes like Gershwin. Instead, he composed memorable melodies – but not too many of them, with only around fifty of his works published during his lifetime.

Barber is remembered today chiefly for his *Adagio for Strings*, which was used by Oliver Stone in his Vietnam War movie, *Platoon*; and for his *Violin Concerto*, which gives the soloist a particularly tough workout in its final movement.

Something of a 'one-hit wonder', **Joaquín Rodrigo** (1901–1999) is famous for his *Concierto* *de Aranjuez.* He composed extensively for the guitar, although he was not actually a guitarist himself. His music did much to make it acceptable to treat the guitar as a serious classical instrument, appearing alongside the orchestra. Rodrigo was helped in this mission by two excellent exponents of his work: the British guitarist Julian Bream and the Australian guitarist John Williams. (Don't confuse this John Williams with the American composer of the same name; we meet the latter on page 232.)

Rodrigo's music is filled with sunny Spanish tunes and, although he is remembered in the main for just one piece, his output was prodigious. He became blind at the age of three years, and composed all of his music using Braille. He always said that, had he not been blind, he would never have become a composer.

William Walton (1902–1983) took over Edward Elgar's crown as the composer that the Establishment loved the most. Born in Oldham, Walton spent a good deal of his childhood at Christ Church, Oxford, where he was a boy chorister. After studying music at Oxford University, he was lucky enough to find himself taken under the wing of the Sitwell family, an artistic and literary tribe, who took care of all his financial needs, allowing him to compose without having money worries.

When Walton was nineteen, he wrote *Façade* as an accompaniment to Edith Sitwell's rather outlandish and highly theatrical poetry. In his twenties, he wrote two of his other most important works – his *Viola Concerto* and *Belshazzar's Feast*, a breathtaking oratorio, which was premiered in Leeds.

Walton became a renowned film composer in the 1940s, and his Shakespearean collaborations with Laurence Olivier were particularly admired. He also wrote marches such as *Crown Imperial* and *Orb and Sceptre* for major state occasions.

Dmitri Shostakovich (1906–1975) was another composer who, like William Walton, wrote a whole body of film soundtracks, including the very famous *'Romance'* from *The Gadfly* and the less well-known *The Assault on Beautiful Gorky.*

Shostakovich was a graduate of the St Petersburg Conservatoire, where his *Symphony No. 1*, written while he was still a student, was hailed as a masterpiece. He fell foul of the state, though, first in 1930 with *The Nose*, condemned by the Communist regime for its 'bourgeois decadence', and then in 1936 Stalin stormed out of a performance of his opera *Lady Macbeth of the Mtsensk District*. The review in the following day's *Pravda* was headed: 'Chaos instead of Music'. And the reviewer went on to brand Shostakovich as 'an enemy of the people'.

Shostakovich penned his *Symphony No. 5*, which is subtitled 'A Soviet Artist's Practical Creative Reply to Just Criticism', as a way of trying to get back into favour. It worked, and he was welcomed back into the fold, although he still had run-ins with the authorities later in his career, and he was creatively free once again only when Stalin died in 1953.

Shostakovich's music could be light and frothy, for example his *Jazz Suites*; or dark and dramatic, for example his *Symphony No. 7*. This epic work tells the story of the siege of Leningrad by the German army.

One interesting aside: Shostakovich also holds the distinction of having one of his songs sung by the cosmonaut Yuri Gagarin over the radio from his spacecraft to mission control down on planet earth.

Our next composer falls into the same category as Schoenberg. **John Cage** (1912–1992) is not somebody whose music we often play on Classic FM. Again, this is because our listeners tell us that they are not overly fond of it. However, he was a big figure in twentieth-century classical music, so he does deserve a mention in these pages.

Cage was one of the major experimentalists of classical music. He made it his life's work to explore different sounds that did not follow any of the rules that had developed over the years that this book covers. His music could be completely simple, or terribly complicated and chaotic.

Cage even created a new instrument – a 'prepared piano' – where pieces of metal and rubber are inserted into the body of the piano to create a completely different sound. He also used electronic tape in some of his pieces.

Cage's most notorious work is called 4'33" and is made up of four and a half minutes of absolute silence, where the pianist sits staring at the piano keyboard without playing a note. The 'music' is then supposed to be whatever other noises are heard in the background in the concert hall. Those in the know hail this as a magnificent concept. We think they may have missed out on having the story of

The Emperor's New Clothes read to them when they were children.

Born in Lowestoft, **Benjamin Britten** (1913–1976) had a consuming love of the county of Suffolk, spending the last thirty years of his life in the seaside village of Aldeburgh, where he began the Aldeburgh Festival in 1948. This is still one of England's annual musical highlights today. Britten lived with his lifelong partner, the tenor Peter Pears, for whom he wrote leading roles in many of his works.

Britten specialised in writing opera and vocal music, with the opera *Peter Grimes*, and his *War Requiem*, written for the consecration of the new Coventry Cathedral, being among his most highly regarded works. However, his most widely heard piece today could not be more different. *The Young Person's Guide to the Orchestra* was written as an introduction to each section of the orchestra for a documentary film made by the Crown Film Unit. Its original name was *Variations and Fugue on a Theme of Henry Purcell* – and the theme in question was taken from the incidental music that Purcell wrote for a play called *Abdelazar*.

Britten provided one of the best analogies we

have seen to describe how composers go about their business: 'Composing is like driving down a foggy road towards a house. Slowly, you see more details of the house – the colour of the slates and bricks, the shape of the windows. The notes are the bricks and mortar of the house.'

Even though Britten was the first composer to be made a life peer, he could be surprisingly unstuffy about what life as a composer was really like: 'The old idea . . . of a composer suddenly having a terrific idea and sitting up all night to write is nonsense. Night time is for sleeping.'

A larger-than-life character and a brilliant musician, **Leonard Bernstein's** (1918–1990) big tuneful hits could not have been more different from the music written by his fellow American John Cage.

Bernstein was an accomplished pianist and a brilliant conductor, touring the world, working with the best orchestras, and spending eleven years as the principal conductor of the New York Philharmonic Orchestra. Bernstein was a master of composition and could as easily write a big populist Broadway hit such as *West Side Story* as he could create a beautifully poignant choral work such as *Chichester Psalms*.

Bernstein was also the first composer to become a television and radio star, and, always passionate about music education, he hosted regular 'Young People's Concerts' for much of his life.

When Bernstein conducted major concerts, his assistant would stand in the wings with a glass of whisky in one hand, a towel in the other, and a lit cigarette in his mouth. As soon as Bernstein finished his performance, he would rush off stage covered in sweat. He would grab the towel and wipe his face; down the Scotch in one, and then take a huge drag on the cigarette, before charging back into the hall to rapturous applause from his adoring public.

Handy 20th-Century Playlist

1   Claude Debussy: *Clair de lune* from *Suite bergamasque*
2   Claude Debussy: *La mer*
3   Claude Debussy: *Prélude à l'après-midi d'un faune*
4   Erik Satie: *Gymnopédies*
5   Erik Satic: *Gnossiennes*
6   Maurice Ravel: *Boléro*
7   Maurice Ravel: *Pavane pour une infante défunte*

8 Maurice Ravel: *Daphnis et Chloé*

9 Maurice Ravel: *Piano Concerto in D for the left hand*

10 Maurice Ravel: *Le tombeau de Couperin*

11 Ralph Vaughan Williams: *Fantasia on a Theme by Thomas Tallis*

12 Ralph Vaughan Williams: *The Lark Ascending*

13 Ralph Vaughan Williams: *English Folksong Suite*

14 Ralph Vaughan Williams: *Fantasia on Greensleeves*

15 Ralph Vaughan Williams: *Symphony No. 2 ('London')*

16 Ralph Vaughan Williams: *Symphony No. 5*

17 Gustav Holst: *The Planets*

18 Gustav Holst: *St Paul's Suite*

19 Frederick Delius: *La Calinda*

20 Frederick Delius: *On Hearing the First Cuckoo in Spring*

21 Frederick Delius: *The Walk to the Paradise Garden*

22 Gerald Finzi: *Eclogue*

23 Fritz Kreisler: *Schön Rosmarin*

24 Percy Grainger: *Music for an English Country Garden*

25 Arnold Schoenberg: *Verklärte Nacht*

26 Béla Bartók: *Concerto for Orchestra*

27 Zoltán Kodály: *Háry János Suite*

28 Franz Lehár: *Gold and Silver Waltz*

29 Alexander Glazunov: *The Seasons*

30 Igor Stravinsky: *The Rite of Spring*

31 Igor Stravinsky: *The Firebird*

32 Sergei Prokofiev: *Romeo and Juliet*

33 Sergei Prokofiev: *Lieutenant Kijé*

34 Sergei Prokofiev: *Peter and the Wolf*

35 Sergei Prokofiev: *Symphony No. 1 ('Classical')*

36 Sergei Prokofiev: *The Love for Three Oranges*

37 Ottorino Respighi: *Pines of Rome*

38 Ermanno Wolf-Ferrari: *Intermezzo* from *Susanna's Secret*

39 Aram Khachaturian: *Adagio* from *Spartacus*

40 Francis Poulenc: *The Story of Babar, the Little Elephant*

41 Francis Poulenc: *Organ Concerto*

42 Francis Poulenc: *Les biches*

43 Jean Françaix: *Malabar Jasmine* from *L'horloge de flore (The Flower Clock)*

44 John Philip Sousa: *The Washington Post*

45 George Gershwin: *Rhapsody in Blue*

46 George Gershwin: *Piano Concerto*

47 George Gershwin: *Porgy and Bess*

48 George Gershwin: *An American in Paris*

49 Aaron Copland: *Fanfare for the Common Man*

50 Aaron Copland: *Rodeo*

51 Aaron Copland: *Simple Gifts* from
    Appalachian Spring

52 Samuel Barber: *Adagio for Strings*

53 Samuel Barber: *Violin Concerto*

54 Joaquín Rodrigo: *Concierto de Aranjuez*

55 Joaquín Rodrigo: *Fantasia para un
    gentilhombre*

56 William Walton: *Spitfire Prelude and Fugue*

57 William Walton: *Crown Imperial*

58 William Walton: *Orb and Sceptre*

59 William Walton: *Belshazzar's Feast*

60 William Walton: *Viola Concerto*

61 William Walton: *Façade*

62 Dmitri Shostakovich: *Jazz Suites Nos 1 and 2*

63 Dmitri Shostakovich: *Romance* from
    The Gadfly

64 Dmitri Shostakovich: *The Assault on Beautiful
    Gorky*

65 Dmitri Shostakovich: *Symphony No. 5*

66 Dmitri Shostakovich: *Piano Concerto No. 2*

67 John Cage: *Sonatas and Interludes*

68 Benjamin Britten: *The Young Person's Guide to the Orchestra*

69 Benjamin Britten: *Four Sea Interludes* from *Peter Grimes*

70 Benjamin Britten: *Ceremony of Carols*

71 Leonard Bernstein: *Candide*

72 Leonard Bernstein: *Chichester Psalms*

73 Leonard Bernstein: *West Side Story*

eight

The 21st Century

Today's Best Music

You could argue that the division between the twentieth-century and the twenty-first-century composers is purely an arbitrary one. It would be true to say that many of the composers who follow enjoyed great success during the twentieth century. However, we wanted to make a distinction in this book that you will not find in many other histories of classical music.

All the composers we feature in this chapter have composed a significant body of work in the twentieth century. All of them have also made a contribution to twenty-first-century classical music, so we believe that, with the benefit of historical perspective, divisions between twentieth-century and twenty-first-century composing may well be made. We're too close in terms of time to be sure where the musical historians of the future will place the dividing line between the end of one period of classical music and the beginning of the next, but we are sure that this line will be drawn, just as it has been in each of the periods we have covered in this book, right back to Early Music times.

When **Peter Maxwell Davies** (1934–) was made Master of the Queen's Music in 2004, he followed a long line of illustrious composers in the job, including Edward Elgar.

Known to everyone simply as 'Max', Davies studied at the Royal Manchester College with a group of young British composers, such as **Harrison Birtwistle** (1934–) , who were together labelled the 'Manchester School'.

Davies studied in Italy and the USA before returning to England as a school teacher. During his long career, he has written many works specifically for performance by school children. As well as an opera, *Taverner*, based on the life of the John Taverner we heard about back on page 12, he has also written a stunning *Antarctic Symphony*, inspired by the time he spent literally at the bottom of the world.

Desolate landscapes must particularly appeal to Davies because he has lived on Orkney since 1971, with the islands and the sea providing huge musical inspiration over the years since. His most popular work among Classic FM listeners is *Farewell to Stromness*, a solo piano piece written as a protest against a nuclear reprocessing plant on one of the Orkney Isles.

The fame of **Henryk Górecki** (1933–2010) rests on one particular work, his *Symphony No. 3*, which has the subtitle *'Symphony of Sorrowful Songs'*. The recording made by the soprano Dawn Upshaw and the London Sinfonietta proved to be a massive hit back in 1992, when Classic FM began broadcasting, although it had actually been composed and received its premiere some fifteen years earlier. The words sung by the soprano, which Górecki set to music in the second movement of this symphony, were written on a cell wall of the Nazi Gestapo's headquarters by a young girl in the Second World War. The result is achingly beautiful and can be extraordinarily moving for the listener.

Originally a primary school teacher, Górecki switched to studying music and in the early part of his career, he wrote many pieces that were quite experimental in their sound and very different from his later work. He had a strong religious belief, which particularly came to the fore in his music in the latter part of his life.

One quick note on his surname: it's not pronounced as it looks. The correct way of saying it is 'Goretski'.

If we were to start to try to identify 'schools' from within our twenty-first-century composers, then we would find that Henryk Górecki's music sits very comfortably alongside that of **Arvo Pärt** (1935–) and **John Tavener** (1944–2013). All three men made their names by composing ethereal-sounding choral music, which has its roots in their religious faith. Their album releases have been commercially successful, but this has come about more through listeners making a spiritual connection with the music than through any form of rampant consumerism on the part of the composers.

Pärt is the only Estonian composer in this book; he studied in the country's capital city, Talinn, doubling up as a recording engineer for Estonian Radio and writing film music in his free time. Pärt's earlier work was quite a tough listen, but in 1969 he stopped composing altogether for seven years after joining the Russian Orthodox Church. When he started writing again, his music took on the style that we know and love today. With its very clean, crisp sound, it has a sparseness about it, which makes it hauntingly beautiful – and extremely relaxing as well.

Another religious man, John Tavener was a member of the Orthodox Christian faith. His music drew on the traditions of this religion, as well as Islamic and Indian music.

John Tavener's composing career began while he was a pupil at Highgate School in north London. His early school compositions were instrumental in winning him a scholarship to the Royal Academy of Music when he was eighteen. There, he met and was influenced by Stravinsky.

Remarkably, Tavener owes some of his early success to Ringo Starr. Tavener's brother was doing some building work for the legendary drummer and gave him a copy of Tavener's *The Whale*. Starr liked it so much that it was released on The Beatles' own Apple record label.

Tavener's music reached its widest audience many years later when his *Song for Athene* was used at the funeral service held at Westminster Abbey for Diana, Princess of Wales, in 1997.

Tavener often composed with a particular performer in mind, and he wrote a number of works specifically for the soprano Patricia Rozario to sing. *The Protecting Veil*, one of his relatively few non-vocal works, was written for the cellist Steven Isserlis.

We have said it before, but it bears saying again. Don't confuse him with the John Taverner who was born in 1490. The clue as to who is who is in the spelling.

During his long and distinguished career, **Philip Glass** (1937–) has been successful at just about any type of classical music he has turned his hand to.

Glass studied at the Juilliard School in New York and also in Paris, before spending time learning about Indian music, a tradition that continues to fascinate him.

Glass is one of the driving forces behind minimalism, alongside **Steve Reich** (1936–) and **Terry Riley** (1935–). This style of music is deceptively simple, often with a few notes repeated over and over again. The effect can be totally mesmerising for the listener.

Much of Glass's music has been first performed by his own group, the Philip Glass Ensemble, but he has also written for orchestras, with his *Violin Concerto* being by far his most widely heard concert work. His soundtrack for Stephen Daldry's film *The Hours* was another great success.

Enormously popular, **John Rutter's** (1945–) music is probably performed more often in more places than any other twenty-first-century composer. His bright and tuneful choral music has made him particularly famous across Britain and the USA. He has specialised in writing Christmas music to such an extent that it is now unusual to go to a carol concert and not hear at least one of his settings.

Like Peter Maxwell Davies, Rutter has often written music specifically to be performed by youngsters. His *Requiem*, which is arguably his greatest work, has become particularly popular with amateur singing groups, and the printed parts for this work are in constant demand by choirs and choral societies across Britain and the USA.

Based in Cambridge, Rutter founded the

Cambridge Singers in 1979. They have since given many of the greatest performances of his work.

Michael Nyman (1944–) coined the term 'Minimalism' while he was putting his own composition work on the back-burner for a while, concentrating instead on musicology and music criticism. It was while he was writing for the *Spectator* that he applied the epithet to the music of Steve Reich and Philip Glass. Nyman is a prolific and commercially successful English composer, having studied at the Royal Academy of Music in the 1960s, where his compositions at the time were at the cutting edge of new music. He went on to study at King's College in London, where he turned back the clock, specialising in seventeenth-century musicology. After that period where he concentrated more on writing words than music, he found that gradually the music was demanding more and more of his time. He formed a highly successful professional partnership with the film director Peter Greenaway, which saw him composing soundtracks for movies such as *The Draughtsman's Contract* and *The Cook, The Thief, His Wife and Her Lover*. However, it is the beautiful music that Nyman composed for Jane

Campion's film *The Piano* that has gained him his greatest and most enduring acclaim.

Another highly commercially successful composer, the Welshman **Karl Jenkins** (1944–) has written music that Classic FM listeners have taken straight to their hearts. He has regularly been the highest-ranked living British composer in our annual Classic FM Hall of Fame charts.

After studying at the University of Wales and at the Royal Academy of Music, Jenkins began his career performing jazz and was a member of the 1970s band Soft Machine. He then moved into writing music for television adverts, winning many awards in the process.

It is as a classical composer that Jenkins is now famed. *Adiemus: Songs of Sanctuary* was the work that first propelled him to the top of the charts – a rare feat for any contemporary classical composer. Its catchy and instantly recognisable style made this fusion of choral and orchestral music a success around the world – it has notched up seventeen platinum or gold album awards. Latterly, *Adiemus* has been eclipsed by another of Jenkins' works in 2000, *The Armed Man: A Mass for Peace*, which has a particularly beautiful cello solo in its *'Benedictus'*.

His *Requiem* was first performed in 2005 and his *Stabat Mater* in 2008. His ear for a tune is second to none and he has proven time and time again that he has the ability to write modern classical music that strikes a chord with twenty-first-century listeners.

Born in New York, the conductor and composer **Carl Davis** (1936–) has made the UK his home since the early 1960s. He is married to the actress Jean Boht, who became a huge star thanks to the television sitcom *Bread*. Davis is no stranger to the small screen either, having written scores for a huge range of different programmes including the 1970s epic *The World at War*. He has also composed ballets and for the theatre (including for the Royal Shakespeare Company) and regularly produces film soundtracks, with a specialism in creating new scores for silent classics. As a conductor, Davis often appears with many orchestras around the UK and is a regular with both the London Philharmonic Orchestra and the Royal Liverpool Philharmonic Orchestra.

In 1990, Davis worked with **Paul McCartney** (1942–) on his *Liverpool Oratorio*. Think Paul McCartney and you don't necessarily think 'classical composer', but the former Beatle has carved out a successful classical music career alongside his rock and pop work. He has always had a knack for writing highly melodic music, and this is apparent throughout his classical pieces.

His *Liverpool Oratorio,* which received its premiere in Liverpool Cathedral in 1991, was his first full-length foray into the world of classical music. McCartney followed this up with *Working Classical*, an album of orchestral and chamber music, and *Standing Stone*, which revisited his earlier successes working with a choir and orchestra. At the end of 2006, McCartney released a new classical work, *'Ecce Cor Meum'*, an oratorio in four movements. Five years later, his first ballet, *Ocean's Kingdom*, received its premiere in New York.

An item of trivia for you: extracts from Beethoven's *Symphony No. 9* and Wagner's *Lohengrin* are both included in The Beatles' movie *Help!*

Ludovico Einaudi (1955–) not only composes music, but he also gets on the road and performs it, with a particularly strong fan base in Britain, Germany and his native Italy. He trained in Milan, before being taught by the respected Italian composer **Luciano Berio** (1925–2003).

Einaudi's popularity is based largely on his solo piano albums; *Le Onde*, which was inspired by Virginia Woolf's novel *The Waves*; and by *I Giorni*, which followed on from his travels around Africa, particularly in Mali. He has also written soundtracks for a number of Italian films.

We jump back to the USA for our next composer, who was born in New York to Hungarian immigrant parents. The Greenwich Village upbringing of **Jay Ungar** (1946–) might seem a million miles from the Catskill strains of his famous hit tune, *The Ashokan Farewell*. In actual fact, the moving melody, originally a country waltz, was written for fond-felt final nights at his annual Fiddle and Dance Camp, run out of the Ashokan Campus of New York State University. It came to prominence after being used in Ken Burn's television films *The Civil War*, and its arrangement by Captain J. R. Perkins, then of the Band of Her Majesty's Royal Marines, propelled it to the higher echelons of the Classic FM Hall of Fame.

Joby Talbot (1971–) was Classic FM's first Composer in Residence. The album *Once Around the Sun* was the culmination of that year-long project.

A graduate of the Guildhall School of Music and Drama in London, Talbot was a member of the pop band The Divine Comedy before turning to the composition of classical music, and film and television scores.

Talbot's film work includes scores for Alfred Hitchcock's *The Lodger* and for *The Hitchhiker's Guide to the Galaxy*, with his television work including the scores to *Robbie the Reindeer* and *The League of Gentlemen*.

Patrick Hawes (1958–) took over from Joby Talbot as Classic FM's Composer in Residence in 2006, with his commissions for the radio station gathered together on the album *Into the Light*. In recent years, Hawes has emerged as one of the most popular contemporary English composers.

Hawes' debut album, *Blue in Blue*, made the fastest ever appearance of any work in the Classic FM Hall of Fame, entering the upper reaches of the chart just months after it was released. His beautiful choral piece 'Quanta qualia' has proved to be a particularly big hit, as has his *Highgrove Suite*, a work commissioned by HRH The Prince of Wales, which received its premiere in 2010.

Hawes' music follows the English Romantic tradition of Delius and Vaughan Williams, although Hawes has a particular interest in Renaissance and Baroque music – a subject that he studied at Durham University.

The strong composing credentials of **Howard Goodall** (1958–) were first established in musical theatre, although he has become among our most successful film and television composers, with credits including *Blackadder*, *Mr Bean*, *Red Dwarf*, *The Catherine Tate Show*, *QI* and *The Vicar of Dibley.* However, it is for his choral music that he is best known to Classic FM listeners. He took over as the station's third Composer in Residence in 2008, relinquishing the role in 2015. He also hosted a regular weekly programme on the station during this period.

Goodall wrote *Enchanted Voices*, an album based on the Beatitudes, which stormed to the top of the Specialist Classical Charts on its release and stayed there for months, winning a Gramophone Award in the process. Goodall was named Composer of the Year at the Classical BRIT Awards in 2009, following the release of *Eternal Light: A Requiem*, which was incorporated into a ballet by the Ballet Rambert.

He has become a familiar face on television, regularly presenting programmes about music and the arts for Channel 4, ITV, Sky Arts and the BBC. He has long been a passionate advocate of the benefits of music education and was England's first National Singing Ambassador.

Other contemporary classical composers who consistently gain critical acclaim include: **James Macmillan** (1959–), possibly the best-known Scottish composer of his generation. His *Veni, Veni Emanuel*, a concerto for percussion first performed in 1992 by Evelyn Glennie, is considered a modern classic. **Judith Weir** (1954–) was named in 2014 as the new Master of the Queen's Music, taking over the role from Peter Maxwell Davies. A former pupil of John Tavener, the opera house and theatre are ideal places to experience her fresh modern sounds. **George Benjamin** (1960–) studied with Messiaen, before having an early contemporary classical hit with *Ringed by the Flat Horizon*. **Gavin Bryars** (1943–) is the most famous – and quite possibly the only famous – composer from Goole in East Yorkshire. His *Jesus' Blood Never Failed Me Yet* was a big hit in the mid-1990s. **Mark-Anthony Turnage** (1960–) is another man at home with composing for the theatre. His opera based on Steven Berkoff's *Greek* is breathtaking.

The American composer **Eric Whitacre** (1970–) began his formal music training at the University of Nevada. He was particularly struck by the music of Mozart – and his *Requiem* in particular. He went on to study composition at the Juilliard School, regarded by many as the USA's preeminent performing arts academy. He first came to prominence in the minds of British audiences with the release of his album *Cloudburst* on the Hyperion record label. This all-choral disc features performances from the choir Polyphony, conducted by Stephen Layton. It includes the eponymous hit written when Whitacre was just twenty-two years old, as well as *'Lux Aurumque'* and *'Sleep'*.

His first album as both a composer and conductor was entitled *Light and Gold* and was released by Decca Records in 2010. It won a Grammy Award and shot to the top of the classical charts in both the UK and USA. He made easy work of the traditionally 'difficult second album', with his follow-up release for Decca, *Water Night*, topping both the iTunes and Billboard classical charts on the day of release. Performances here were from his newly assembled professional choir, the Eric Whitacre Singers.

Whitacre has sprung to fame online because of his innovative 'Virtual Choir' project, which has garnered millions of YouTube views, after thousands of singers from around the world were invited to upload their own performances of Whitacre tracks, which were then mixed together to create a unique online performance.

The first of a trio in a new generation of young British choral composers, **Paul Mealor** (1975–) sprang into the nation's musical consciousness at the biggest event of 2011 – the wedding of the Duke and Duchess of Cambridge at Westminster Abbey. His motet *Ubi Caritas* was heard by 2.5 billion people around the world – the largest television audience in broadcasting history. At the end of 2011, he was a darling of the media once again after composing the music to *'Wherever You Are'*, a choral work that stormed to the top of the charts after being recorded by the Military Wives. This choir, made up of wives and girlfriends of soldiers serving in Afghanistan, was put together by the inspirational choirmaster Gareth Malone.

Mealor studied music at the University of York

and combines his work as a choral composer with life as an academic at the University of Aberdeen. The best collection of his music to date comes on the album *A Tender Light,* where it is performed by the choir Tenebrae under the direction of Nigel Short.

The same choir has recorded two notable albums featuring the music of **Will Todd** (1970–). He gives the prodigious composers of old a run for their money, writing his first work when he was just seven years old. As well as writing for choirs, he also composes for the stage and for orchestras and his music is gaining in popularity across Europe and the USA. Tenebrae, with Nigel Short conducting, recorded his *The Call of Wisdom* in 2012, with their *Lux et Veritas* release one of the standout classical albums of 2014.

Philip Stopford (1977–) had no fewer than three separate entries in the 2014 Classic FM Hall of Fame. He is best known for his setting of *'Ave verum corpus'* – *'Ave Verum'* – and also of the *Coventry Carol* titled *'Lully, Lulla, Lullay'.* He was himself a chorister at Westminster Abbey, before studying music at Keble College, Oxford. He is the Director of the choir Ecclesium, having previously been the Choral Director of St Anne's Cathedral in Belfast.

Handy 21st-Century Playlist

1   Peter Maxwell Davies: *Farewell to Stromness*
2   Henryk Górecki: *Symphony No. 3*
3   Arvo Pärt: *Spiegel im Spiegel*
4   John Tavener: *The Protecting Veil*
5   John Tavener: *The Lamb*
6   John Tavener: *Song for Athene*
7   John Rutter: *Requiem*
8   John Rutter: *A Gaelic Blessing*
9   John Rutter: *For the Beauty of the Earth*
10 Philip Glass: *Violin Concerto*
11 Philip Glass: *Koyaanisqatsi*
12 Philip Glass: *The Hours*
13 Philip Glass: *Kundun*
14 Michael Nyman: *The Piano*
15 Karl Jenkins: *Adiemus: Songs of Sanctuary*
16 Karl Jenkins: *Palladio*
17 Karl Jenkins: *'Benedictus'* and *'Sanctus'* from
    The Armed Man: A Mass for Peace
18 Carl Davis: *The World at War*
19 Carl Davis: *The French Lieutenant's Woman*
20 Paul McCartney: *Liverpool Oratorio*

21 Paul McCartney: *Standing Stone*

22 Ludovico Einaudi: *Le Onde*

23 Ludovico Einaudi: *I Giorni*

24 Jay Ungar: *The Ashokan Farewell*

25 Joby Tolbot: *Once Around the Sun*

26 Patrick Hawes: *Blue in Blue*

27 Patrick Hawes: *Into the Light*

28 Patrick Hawes: *Highgrove Suite*

29 Howard Goodall: *The Lord is My Shepherd*

30 Howard Goodall: *Enchanted Voices*

31 Howard Goodall: *Eternal Light: A Requiem*

32 Eric Whitacre: *The Seal Lullaby*

33 Paul Mealor: *'Ubi Caritas'*

34 Will Todd: *'Lux et Veritas'*

35 Philip Stopford: *'Ave Verum'*

Classical Music at the Cinema

Here, we jump slightly out of the chronological sequence that we have tried to preserve as best we can throughout the pages of this book. Film composers straddle both the twentieth and twenty-first century and it seems more logical to bring them together in one section. In a moment, we shall also discuss the film soundtrack's newer, younger sibling, the videogame soundtrack.

There are two types of classical music used in films: the first is when a film director borrows an existing classical work and uses it to complement the pictures and the second happens when a brand new music score is commissioned especially for the movie.

Some of the most famous examples of the former include Rachmaninov's *Piano Concerto No. 2*, which features in *Brief Encounter*; Mozart's *Clarinet Concerto* in *Out of Africa*; Richard Strauss's *Also Sprach Zarathustra* in *2001: A Space Odyssey*; and even Mozart's *Eine kleine Nachtmusik* in the unlikely setting of *Ace Ventura: Pet Detective*.

In *Fantasia*, Walt Disney created a whole animated film with a score provided by the classical greats, including Bach, Beethoven, Dukas, Ponchielli, Mussorgsky, Tchaikovsky, Schubert and Stravinsky. There was even a live-action role for the Philadelphia Orchestra and their conductor Leopold Stokowski. On seeing the section featuring the *Pastoral Symphony*, Walt Disney is reported to have said, 'Gee! That'll make Beethoven!'

The very first film soundtrack ever written was composed by Saint-Saëns for the 1908 movie *L'Assassinat du duc de Guise*. Since then, a whole list of mainstream classical composers have written specifically for the silver screen, including Malcolm Arnold, Benjamin Britten, Aaron Copland, Philip Glass, Aram Khachaturian, Eric Korngold, Sergei Prokofiev, Dmitri Shostakovich, Ralph Vaughan Williams and William Walton. The link between film soundtracks and classical music is irrefutable – in many ways, it is a natural development of the long tradition of composers writing incidental music to accompany stage plays.

There are many important composers who have made their names writing specifically for the big screen throughout the twentieth century and since the turning of the new millennium. Here are some of those whom we hear most often on Classic FM.

Richard Addinsell (1904–1977) penned the *Warsaw Concerto* as a pastiche of a Romantic piano concerto for the 1941 film *Dangerous Moonlight*, as well as the scores for *Goodbye Mr Chips* and *The Prince and the Showgirl*. The Italian **Ennio Morricone** (1928–) began his professional life playing in a jazz band, but ended up scoring films ranging from *The Mission* to *The Good, The Bad and the Ugly*. **Elmer Bernstein** (1922–2004) was one of the heavyweights of the soundtrack world, penning such delights as the music to *The Magnificent Seven*, while **Max Steiner** (1888–1971) wrote the theme for *Gone with the Wind*. And then there was **Eric Coates** (1886–1957), who gave us *The Dambusters March* – work that, in fact, he had already written before the film came along. He just needed somewhere to put it. **Jerry Goldsmith** (1929–2004) was another of the giants of the film-music world; his scores range from *Star Trek* to *The Omen*. In terms of scary soundtracks, it would be impossible to miss out **Bernard Herrmann** (1911–1975) and the music to *Psycho* from any comprehensive list.

Craig Armstrong (1959–), who wrote the music for the 1996 film *William Shakespeare's Romeo and Juliet*, and **Patrick Doyle** (1953–), the man behind *Sense and Sensibility*, are among Scotland's most successful film composers. England offers **Nigel Hess** (1953–), who penned *Ladies in Lavender*; **Rachel Portman** (1960–), who did the honours with *Chocolat*; **Stephen Warbeck** (1953–), the composer of *Shakespeare in Love*; and **Debbie Wiseman** (1963–), who enjoyed a big hit with the soundtrack to *Wilde*. Meanwhile, Italy's

Dario Marianelli (1963–) won an Oscar for the music he composed for *Atonement*. **Klaus Badelt** (1967–) is one of a new generation of film composers, with his theme for *Pirates of the Caribbean* being especially well known to current movie-goers.

John Williams (1932–) is the undisputed king of celluloid composition. So far, he has written the music for more than a hundred different movies. And there is no doubt that the rest of the film industry appreciates his talents: he has forty-nine Oscar nominations (the highest number for any living person), carrying off the statuette five times. He has been nominated for twenty-five Golden Globes, winning four times. Of his fifty-nine Grammy Award nominations, he was victorious on twenty-one occasions. His mantelpiece must by now need some sort of structural reinforcement, such is the weight of his accolades.

Williams was born in New York, moving with his family to Los Angeles in 1948. He had loved music from when he was a boy and, after finishing his first set of studies, he joined the American Air Force. Next, Williams moved back to New York for more studying, this time at the world-famous Juilliard School. In the evenings, he made money working as a pianist in many of the jazz clubs in the city's Manhattan area.

Finally, Williams made the move back to Los Angeles, where he started to work in the film and television industry. Throughout the 1960s, he wrote the theme tunes of many successful American television programmes. Then, in 1973, Williams met the film director Steven Spielberg, with whom he has subsequently enjoyed the greatest creative partnership of his long career. Their first film was called *Sugarland Express*. Since then, their list of credits includes blockbuster after blockbuster. Williams also collaborated very successfully with the *Star Wars* director, George Lucas, working on all six films in the series.

Despite the fact that he could choose to write his music using a computer programme, Williams prefers the old-fashioned way of composing. He uses a piano to work out the tune, and a pencil and paper to write down what he has composed. It's hard work, too – he might have only eight weeks to write around two hours of music for a full orchestra for a film.

Until his death, **John Barry** (1933–2011) was Britain's answer to John Williams. Born in

York, where his father owned a cinema business, Barry was always fascinated by the movies. His film soundtracks, spanning more than thirty years, include *Zulu*, *The Ipcress File*, *Born Free*, *Midnight Cowboy*, *King Kong*, *The Deep*, *Chaplin* and *Indecent Proposal*.

Barry is probably best known for his work on the James Bond films *From Russia with Love*, *Goldfinger*, *Thunderball*, *You Only Live Twice*, *On Her Majesty's Secret Service*, *Diamonds Are Forever*, *The Man with the Golden Gun*, *Octopussy*, *A View to a Kill* and *The Living Daylights*.

Barry's greatest classical scores are *Out of Africa* from 1985 and *Dances with Wolves* from 1990. It is no accident that both these films feature wide open landscape photography – just the sort of images that blend perfectly with Barry's lush epic scores. The director of *Out of Africa*, Sydney Pollack, said of John Barry, 'You can't listen to his music without seeing movies in your head.' The film earned Barry his fourth Oscar, a Grammy Award for Best Instrumental Composition and a Golden Globe Award. *Dances with Wolves* won him his fifth Oscar and another Grammy Award for Best Instrumental Composition.

The Beyondness of Things was Barry's first album of classical music not written as a film soundtrack. The absence of pictures did nothing to dampen his ability to compose great tunes.

No list of twenty-first-century film composers would be complete without mention of the Canadian **Howard Shore** (1946–). He wrote the soundtracks to all three movies that make up Peter Jackson's *Lord of the Rings* trilogy. When we ask Classic FM listeners to vote for their all-time favourite film soundtracks, it is *Lord of the Rings* that consistently tops the polls. Shore also penned the music for the films in the *Hobbit* trilogy. The soundtracks for the first in the series, *The Hobbit: An Unexpected Journey*, was recorded by the London Philharmonic Orchestra, as they were for all of the *Lord of the Rings* movies, but the New Zealand Symphony Orchestra can be heard on the soundtracks to *The Hobbit: The Desolation of Smaug* and *The Hobbit: The Battle of the Five Armies*.

A little trivia for you: Shore himself is rumoured to make a cameo appearance as a Rohan Guard in the extended DVD edition of *The Lord of the Rings: The Return of the King*.

Born in the USA, **James Horner** (1953–)

started playing the piano when he was five years old and trained at the Royal College of Music in London before moving back to California, where he studied for a series of music degrees, culminating in a doctorate in Music Composition and Theory. Horner's first major film soundtrack was *Star Trek II: The Wrath of Khan* in 1982, and since then he has worked with film directors such as Steven Spielberg, Oliver Stone and Ron Howard, scoring more than a hundred films.

One of the most commercially successful film composers, Horner has won two Oscars, two Golden Globes and three Grammy Awards. He has a further eight Oscar nominations, seven Golden Globe nominations and four Grammy Award nominations to his name. His best-known work by a long, long way is *Titanic*.

A brilliant musician as a child in Frankfurt, **Hans Zimmer** (1957–) began his career in the world of pop music, working with the band The Buggles. Their hit *'Video Killed the Radio Star'* was the first video to be broadcast on MTV.

Zimmer worked as an assistant to the composer **Stanley Myers** (1930–1993) and had early success as the writer of television theme tunes. As a film composer, he has made his name for his skilful combination of electronic music with a traditional orchestral sound. His biggest success has been the soundtrack to *Gladiator*, which has sold more than three million copies around the globe. He also provided the scores for the second, third and fourth films in the hugely successful *Pirates of the Caribbean* franchise.

Handy Film Soundtrack Playlist

1 Howard Shore: *The Lord of the Rings*
2 Hans Zimmer: *Gladiator*
3 John Williams: *Schindler's List*
4 John Barry: *Dances with Wolves*
5 John Barry: *Out of Africa*
6 Klaus Badelt: *Pirates of the Caribbean*
7 John Williams: *Jurassic Park*
8 Ennio Morricone: *The Mission*
9 Elmer Bernstein: *The Magnificent Seven*
10 Nigel Hess: *Ladies in Lavender*
11 John Williams: *Saving Private Ryan*
12 Michael Nyman: *The Piano*
13 John Williams: *E.T.*
14 James Horner: *Titanic*
15 Max Steiner: *Gone with the Wind*

Classical Music on the Games Console

The inclusion of our final section of classical composers might well be controversial in some circles. And it's a musical contretemps that is happening right now – and hasn't quite resolved itself one way or the other.

It is possibly worth pausing for a moment to bring you up to speed, in case you aren't completely *au fait* with the world of video gaming. There has been an explosion of video games produced for consoles such as the Microsoft Xbox and the Sony PlayStation. Many of these games include especially commissioned classical orchestral soundtracks, written by composers who tend to specialise in the genre. The music is composed so that it develops as a player moves through the game. Structurally, many of the ideas are common to other musical forms, so a composer might use a particular theme to accompany action involving a certain character. In terms of the sound world it inhabits, much of this music features the instruments of a traditional symphony orchestra and we would recognise it as being classical music in its style – so, no pounding rock rhythms, disco beats, or cheesy snare-drum accompaniment to orchestral settings. In many ways, the sound is not dissimilar to the most successful symphonic film soundtracks.

Gradually, film soundtracks have come to be regarded as a legitimate part of the overall canon of the classical music repertoire by many classical music performers, listeners and commentators although, it should be said, some people do feel that the genre should be kept separate from the more core compositions, locked away in its own separate room, if you like.

However, not everyone feels quite so positive about soundtracks that have been written for use on video games. We found this out for ourselves when, in 2012, we included votes for video game soundtracks in the Classic FM Hall of Fame. By 2014, the music of **Nobuo Uematsu** (1959–) for the *Final Fantasy* series occupied the No. 7 position in the chart, while *The Elder Scrolls* soundtrack, penned by **Jeremy Soule** (1975–) was at No. 17. Meanwhile, Edinburgh-born composer **Grant Kirkhope** (1962–) had no fewer than three separate entries in our Top 300.

Some of our listeners felt that we were wrong to include music that was composed primarily for use on games consoles, arguing that this wasn't classical music. Other people – most notably those involved in the very active gaming community – were delighted that the music they know and love was being accorded artistic status in its own right. Many listeners who didn't have a strong ideological objection to the concept of video game music being broadcast on a classical music radio station made their judgement on the music itself regardless of its origins – either they liked it or they didn't.

For our part, we tend to fall in this third category. Just as with every other form of music, whether it be classical or rock, pop, dance or jazz, in the genre of video game soundtracks, there are good compositions and bad ones, excellent recordings and poor ones, gripping performances and mediocre ones. So, we don't think that all video game music hits the spot; but there are undoubtedly some very strong compositions that we are delighted to feature as part of Classic FM's extensive playlist.

After all, the composers who are writing this music are following in a long tradition of producing new work to match all of the available means of distribution of the day. The same argument can be made for classical film soundtracks; the only difference here being that film soundtracks have been around for more than a century, but video game music is a much newer art form – and perhaps one with which many classical music enthusiasts have yet to become familiar.

Unsurprisingly, given the importance of the country in the development of video game hardware, Japan led the way in recognising that these soundtracks could be sold as musical works in their own right, away from the game environment. In the UK, the London Philharmonic Orchestra has had huge success with two albums of orchestrations of video game soundtracks conducted by Andrew Skeet. As well as the more recent recordings, these albums include relatively vintage examples of the genre, such as *Sonic the Hedgehog* and *Super Mario*.

Both the London Symphony Orchestra and the Royal Scottish National Orchestra have enjoyed huge success in presenting live concerts of video game music, with full symphony orchestras performing the works as traditional classical concerts in their normal concert hall homes. The Philharmonia Orchestra has developed something of a speciality of recording soundtracks for the games, working with leading composers in the field such as **Mark Griskey** (1963–), **James Hannigan** (1971–) and **Christopher Lennertz** (1972–) on titles as wide-ranging as *Harry Potter*, *The Lord of the Rings* and *Command & Conquer*. Indeed, leading video games companies such as EA Games are now among the more significant commissioners of newly composed symphonic music for orchestras such as the Philharmonia to record today.

And the gradual blending of video game music into the classical music world isn't limited to the orchestral sector here in the UK. The Czech National Symphony Orchestra has presented video game music concerts at the Gewandhaus concert hall in Leipzig; the LA Philharmonic played in the first official *Final Fantasy* concert at the Walt Disney Concert Hall in Los Angeles, and the Malmö Symphonic Orchestra has promoted live concerts featuring music from the world of video games in Sweden. And these examples are just the tip of the iceberg. Without doubt, this is one of the fastest-growing – and fastest-selling – areas of live classical music for the orchestral sector today.

One of the more creatively interesting areas of working with computers is the vast array of possibilities that it opens up for collaboration across art forms. Students at Virginia Tech University in the USA have already seized this opportunity, composing an opera based on the highly successful video game *Minecraft* and the music of Mozart. They have called the new work *OperaCraft*.

No doubt the debate will continue to rage, but we are more than happy to include it in this book because we believe that this is an area of classical music that will rapidly develop over the next few years.

Handy Video Game Soundtrack Playlist

1 Nobuo Uematsu: *Final Fantasy*
2 Jeremy Soule: *The Elder Scrolls*
3 Grant Kirkhope: *Banjo Kazooie*
4 Grant Kirkhope: *Viva Piñata*
5 Grant Kirkhope: *Kingdoms of Amalur*
6 Russell Brower: *World of Warcraft*
7 Yoko Shimomura: *Kingdom Hearts*
8 Austin Wintory: *Journey*

Conclusion

And so there we end our journey through the history of classical music – a journey that has lasted for more than 1,600 years so far, and we are confident that there is plenty more to come.

We started way back with Ambrose and Gregory sorting out the rules of plainchant, and then we travelled through musical time, taking in the Medieval, Renaissance, Baroque, Classical and Romantic periods along the way, ending up with the music of the past hundred years.

Is classical music struggling to find its place in the twenty-first-century world? On the contrary, classical music and the people who compose and perform it are in the rudest of health. It's worth noting that, of the 198 composers whom we've featured in detail in our classical music chronology, 93 of them were alive at some point in the past hundred years. That sounds to us like an art form that is continuing to reinvent itself and to thrive.

The music of the great composers, such as J. S. Bach, Mozart and Beethoven, is as relevant to our lives right now as it was on the day that it was written. One of the most exciting parts of life at Classic FM is the thrill of discovering a work of brilliance, which you can then share with other people. All the time new composers are coming along, writing new pieces that will become central parts of books just like this in the future. At the same time, new young performers are coming to the fore, providing modern interpretations of the music of the great composers, and championing fresh young talent.

Classical music is very much alive and well. It will go on changing its shape and sound for as long as there are people with ears to listen. And, rest assured, Classic FM will be there to share the world's greatest music with you on your radio, on your computer, on your mobile phone, on your tablet, or on a myriad of different devices that have yet to be dreamed up by the next generation of technological whizz-kids. This voyage of classical music discovery will never stop being exciting because none of us can quite predict who or what is just around the corner.

Where To Find Out More

If this series of books has whetted your appetite to find out more, one of the best ways to discover what you like about classical music is to listen to Classic FM. We broadcast a huge breadth of classical music 24 hours a day across the UK on 100–102 FM, on DAB digital radio, online at ClassicFM.com, on Sky channel 0106, on Freeview channel 731, on Virgin Media channel 922 and on FreeSat channel 721. You can also download the free Classic FM App, which will enable you to listen to Classic FM on your iPhone, iPod, iPad, Blackberry or Android device.

As well as being able to listen online, you will find a host of interactive features about classical music, composers and musicians on our website, ClassicFM.com. When we first turned on

Classic FM's transmitters more than two decades ago, we changed the face of classical music radio in the UK for ever. Now, we are doing the same online.

If books are more your thing than websites, then we hope you will enjoy the companion volumes to *Classic FM's Handy Guide to Everything You Ever Wanted to Know About Classical Music*, which are listed at the back of the book. However, if you would like to delve far, far deeper into the subject than we have been able to in this series, the universally acknowledged authority on the subject is *The New Grove Dictionary of Music and Musicians*. The original version was edited by Sir George Grove, with the eminent musicologist Stanley Sadie taking over the reins for editions published since 1980. But be warned – this is a weighty tome, running to 20 hardback volumes with around 29,000 separate articles. A paperback edition was brought out in 1995 and there is also a subscription service online.

In truth, this massive resource is far more detailed than most music lovers would ever need; a more manageable reference book is *The Concise Oxford Dictionary of Music*, edited by Michael Kennedy (published by Oxford Reference), or *The Penguin Companion to Classical Music*, edited by

Paul Griffiths (published by Penguin). Paul Griffiths has also written *A Concise History of Western Music* – a highly readable discussion of the way in which classical music has evolved over time.

The DK Eyewitness Companion to Classical Music, edited by John Burrows (published by Dorling Kindersley), is a very colourful and reliable source of information on the chronology of classical music. Howard Goodall delves into five episodes that changed musical history, including the invention of musical notation and the creation of the recording industry, in his excellent book *Big Bangs* (published by Vintage). Howard also places classical music in the context of the whole of music history in his highly recommended book *The Story of Music* (published by Chatto & Windus). For a slightly quirkier walk through the subject, we would suggest *Stephen Fry's Incomplete & Utter History of Classical Music*, which is published by Macmillan and is based on the award-winning Classic FM radio series of the same name, written by our breakfast show host Tim Lihoreau.

Other excellent general guides to classical music include: *The Rough Guide to Classical Music*, edited by Joe Staines (published by Rough Guides);

The Encyclopedia of Music by Max Wade-Matthews and Wendy Thompson (published by Hermes House); *Good Music Guide* by Neville Garden (published by Columbia Marketing); *The Chronicle of Classical Music* by Alan Kendall (published by Thames & Hudson); *The Lives & Times of the Great Composers* by Michael Steen (published by Icon); *The Lives of the Great Composers* by Harold C. Schonberg (published by Abacus); and *Music for the People: The Pleasures and Pitfalls of Classical Music* by Gareth Malone, whose television series on singing are fast making him a national treasure (published by Collins).

Three excellent books on the subject of opera are *The DK Eyewitness Guide to Opera* (published by Dorling Kindersley); *The Good Opera Guide* by Denis Forman (published by Phoenix); and *The Rough Guide to Opera* by Matthew Boyden (published by Rough Guides).

For younger classical music lovers or discoverers, *The Story of Classical Music* and *Famous Composers* are both published by Naxos Audiobooks. These titles, read by the Classic FM presenter Aled Jones, are aimed at eight- to fourteen-year-olds and contain musical excerpts and CD-ROM elements.

The very best way to find out more about which pieces of classical music you like is by going out and hearing a live performance by one of our great British orchestras for yourself. There is simply no substitute for seeing the whites of the eyes of a talented soloist as he or she performs a masterpiece on stage only a few feet in front of you, alongside a range of hugely accomplished musicians playing together as one.

Classic FM has a series of partnerships with orchestras across the country: the Bournemouth Symphony Orchestra, the London Symphony Orchestra, the Orchestra of Opera North, the Philharmonia Orchestra, the Royal Liverpool Philharmonic Orchestra, the Royal Northern Sinfonia and the Royal Scottish National Orchestra. And don't forget the brilliant young musicians of the National Children's Orchestras of Great Britain and of the National Youth Orchestra of Great Britain. To see if any of these orchestras have a concert coming up near you, log onto our website at ClassicFM.com and click on the 'Concerts and Events' section. It will also include many other classical concerts – both professional and amateur – that are taking place near where you live.

Acknowledgements

Although there is often only one author's name on the cover of a book such as this, writing is very often a team game. And that is very much the case at Classic FM. So, thank you to everyone who works on-air and behind the scenes, each of whom has played an important part in making Classic FM the most successful brand in classical music in the UK today.

The list of credits includes: Alexander Armstrong, Nick Bailey, Jamie Beesley, Catherine Bott, John Brunning, Stuart Campbell, Lucy Chisholm-Batten, Alistair Cockburn, Lucy Coward, Lizzie Davis, Tim Edwards, Simon Funnell, Howard Goodall CBE, Charlotte Green, Sam Jackson, Alex James, Aled Jones MBE, Jane Jones, Will Kisby, Myleene Klass, Kirsty Leith, Laurence

Llewelyn-Bowen, Tim Lihoreau, Kyle Macdonald, James Marshall, David Mellor, Anne-Marie Minhall, Jenny Nelson, Phil Noyce, Bill Overton, Nicholas Owen, Emma Oxborrow, Clare Patterson, Giles Pearman, Tommy Pearson, Sam Pittis, Daniel Ross, Caeshia St Paul, John Suchet, Margherita Taylor, Alan Titchmarsh MBE and Rob Weinberg.

Enormous thanks are also due to Global's Founder and Executive President, Ashley Tabor; to Group Chief Executive, Stephen Miron; to Director of Broadcasting, Richard Park; to Chairman, Lord Allen of Kensington CBE; and to Chief Strategy Officer, Will Harding.

Thank you also to the Elliott & Thompson team of Lorne Forsyth, Olivia Bays, Jennie Condell, Pippa Crane and Thomas Ogilvie for their continued help, support and expertise. Great publishers are hard to find – and they are the best in the business.

About the Author

Darren Henley has spent twenty-five years working in radio, leading Classic FM for fifteen years, first as Managing Editor and then as Managing Director. Named 'Commercial Radio Programmer of the Year' in 2009 and the recipient of the Sir Charles Groves Prize for 'his outstanding contribution to British music', he was appointed an OBE in 2013 for services to music. He has led the development of Classic FM across a range of different platforms, with the creation of the UK's biggest classical music website, innovative new digital products and services, market-leading record labels, live concerts and book publishing.

Darren's two independent government reviews into music education and cultural education, published in 2011 and 2012, resulted in the creation of

England's first National Plan for Music Education, new networks of Music Education Hubs and Heritage Schools, the Museums and Schools programme, the BFI Film Academy and the National Youth Dance Company. He chairs the government's Cultural Education Board and the Mayor of London's Music Education Task Force. He is a trustee of the exam board ABRSM, a Commissioner for the University of Warwick Commission on the Future of Cultural Value, and a board member and vice president of the Canterbury Festival.

Darren is the author of twenty-nine books, including two *Sunday Times* bestsellers. His book *The Virtuous Circle: Why Creativity and Cultural Education Count*, co-written with leading arts educationalists Sir John Sorrell and Paul Roberts, and published by Elliott and Thompson, argues that an excellent cultural education is the right of everyone, bringing personal, social and commercial advantages that can only benefit the lives of all individuals in our society.

A politics graduate from the University of Hull, he is a Fellow of the Royal Society of Arts, the Radio Academy and the London College of Music; an Honorary Fellow of Liverpool John Moores

University, Canterbury Christ Church University and Trinity Laban Conservatoire of Music and Dance; an Honorary Member of the Royal Northern College of Music and the Incorporated Society of Musicians; and a Companion of the Chartered Management Institute. He holds honorary doctorates from the University of Hull, Birmingham City University and Buckinghamshire New University.

Index

Aberdeen, University of 226
Addinsell, Richard 230;
    Goodbye Mr Chips 230;
    *The Prince and the
    Showgirl* 230; *Warsaw
    Concerto* 230
Albéniz, Isaac 119–120;
    Iberia 120
Albinoni, Tomaso 33; *Adagio
    in G minor* 33, 49; *Oboe
    Concerto in D minor,
    Op. 9 No. 2* 49
Aldeburgh Festival 200
Allegri, Gregorio 24–25;
    Miserere 24–25, 48, 64
Ambrose, Bishop 4–5, 245
America *see* USA
Anhalt-Cöthen, Prince
    Leopold of 40
Anne, Queen 43
Arensky, Anton 158

Argentina 47, 120, 121
Armstrong, Craig, *Romeo and
    Juliet* 231
Armstrong, Louis xvi–xvii
Arnold, Malcolm 230
Augustine 4
Auric, Georges 148, 191

Bach, Carl Philipp Emanuel
    40, 55–56; *Harpsichord
    Concerto in D minor* 75
Bach, Johann Christian 40,
    59–60; *Symphonies,
    Op. 3* 75
Bach, Johann Christoph
    39
Bach, Johann Christoph
    Friedrich 40
Bach, Johann Sebastian 29,
    38–42, 55, 59, 62, 122,
    147, 157, 246;

Bach, Johann Sebastian
(CONTD.) *Brandenburg
Concertos* 23, 49;
Goldberg Variations 49;
Prelude No. 1 98; *St John
Passion* 41; *St Matthew
Passion* 41, 49; *The Art
of Fugue* 42; 'The Coffee
Cantata' 41; *Toccata and
Fugue in D minor* 49

Bach, Maria Barbara 39–40

Bach, Wilhelm Friedemann
40

Badelt, Klaus 232; *Pirates of
the Caribbean* 232, 237

Balakirev, Mily 106

ballet 26–27, 55

Ballet Rambert 222

Band of Her Majesty's Royal
Marines 220

Barber, Samuel 196; *Adagio
for Strings* 196, 206;
Violin Concerto 196, 206

Baroque period 2, 21–50,
51, 52, 53, 55, 75, 103,
138, 222, 245

Barry, John 233–234; *A
View to a Kill* 234;
Born Free 234; *Chaplin*
234; *Dances with Wolves*
234, 237; *Diamonds
Are Forever* 234; *From
Russia with Love* 234;
Goldfinger 234; *Indecent*

Proposal 234; *King
Kong* 234; *Midnight
Cowboy* 234; *Octopussy*
234; *On Her Majesty's
Secret Service* 234; *Out
of Africa* 234, 237; *The
Beyondness of Things*
235; *The Deep* 234; *The
Ipcress File* 234; *The
Living Daylights* 234;
*The Man with the Golden
Gun* 234; *Thunderball*
234; *You Only Live Twice*
234; *Zulu* 234

Bartók, Béla 182–183;
Concerto for Orchestra
183, 205

Beatles, The 10, 213, 219

Beecham, Thomas 126, 178

Beethoven, Ludwig van
xv, 38, 52, 56, 62, 68,
69–73, 81, 85, 88, 97,
144, 147, 157, 163,
229, 246; *Bagatelle in
A minor (Für Elise)*
73, 76; *Fidelio* 72,
77; *Piano Concerto
No. 5 ('Emperor')* 77;
*Piano Sonata No. 14
('Moonlight')* 71, 73,
76; *Symphony No. 1*
68; *Symphony No. 5*
76, 90; *Symphony
No. 6 ('Pastoral')* 76,

229; *Symphony No. 9 ('Choral')* 68, 72, 76, 219; *Violin Concerto* 76

Belfast, St Anne's Cathedral 227

Belgium 123, 131

Bellini, Vincenzo 86–87; *Il Pirata* 85; *La Straniera* 86; *Norma* 87, 100

Belyayev, Mitrofan 185

Benedict XVI, Pope 8

Benjamin, George, *Ringed by the Flat Horizon* 223

Berio, Luciano 219

Berkoff, Steven 224

Berlin 91, 123, 189

Berlin, Irving xv

Berlioz, Hector 88–90, 97, 129, 147; *Requiem* 90, 100; *Symphonie fantastique* 89, 100; *The Childhood of Christ* 100

Bernstein, Elmer 230–231; *The Magnificent Seven* 231, 237

Bernstein, Leonard 192, 202–203; *Candide* 207; *Chichester Psalms* 202, 207; *West Side Story* 202, 207

Birmingham Festival 98, 113

Birtwistle, Harrison 210

Bizet, Georges 98–99, 129; *'Au fond du temple saint' (The Pearl Fishers)* 98, 99, 101;

Carmen 98, 99, 101; *Jeux d'enfants* 101; *L'Arlésienne Suite No. 1* 101

Blake, William 124

Boccherini, Luigi 60–61; *Cello Concerto No. 9* 75; *'Minuet' (String Quintet in E)* 60, 75

Boht, Jean 218

Boito, Arrigo 190

Bolivia 47

Borodin, Alexander 105–106, 108; *In the Steppes of Central Asia* 111; *Prince Igor* 106, 111; *String Quartet No. 2* 111

Boston Symphony Orchestra 183

Boulanger, Nadia 192

Bournemouth Symphony Orchestra 253

Boyce, William 53–54, 179; *Symphony No. 4* 75

Bradford 178

Brahms, Johannes 96, 113, 143–145; *Academic Festival Overture* 164; *Hungarian Dance No. 5* 164; *Piano Concerto No. 1* 165; *Quintet in B minor for clarinet and strings* 145; *Symphony No. 4* 165; *Violin Concerto* 165

Braille 197

Brazil 122

Bream, Julian 197

Brindley, James 53

Britain 4, 21, 52, 85, 92, 156, 215, 219

Britten, Benjamin 201–202, 230; *Ceremony of Carols* 207; *Peter Grimes* 201, 207; *The Young Person's Guide to the Orchestra* 207; *Variations and Fugue on a Theme of Henry Purcell* 201; *War Requiem* 201

Brower, Russell, *World of Warcraft* 243

Bruch, Max 145–146, 189; *Kol Nidrei* 146, 165; *Scottish Fantasy* 165; *Symphony No. 3* 165; *Violin Concerto No. 1* 145, 165

Bruckner, Anton 142–143; *Locus Iste* 164; *Symphony in D minor* ('*Die Nullte*') 142; *Symphony in F minor* (*Symphony No. 00*) 142; *Symphony No. 1 in C minor* 142; *Symphony No. 7* 143, 164; *Symphony No. 8* 164

Bryars, Gavin, *Jesus' Blood Never Failed Me Yet* 223

Buggles, The 236

Bull, Ole 116

Burn, Ken 220

Butterworth, George 127

Buxtehude, Dietrich 39

Byrd, William 13–14, 25; '*Ave verum corpus*' 18

Cage, John 199–201, 203; *4'33"* 200–201; *Sonatas and Interludes* 206

Cambrai Cathedral 11

Cambridge 125, 175, 215; Duke and Duchess of 225

Cambridge Singers 216

Campion, Jane 217

Canteloube, Joseph 130

Canterbury 13, 26

Carl Rosa Opera Company 126

castrati 57

Catholic Church/Catholics 4, 8, 12, 13, 14, 24

Chabrier, Emmanuel 130, 148

Chapel Royal 13, 25, 32, 54; Children of the 31

Charles II 31

Charles VI, Emperor 36

Charpentier, Marc-Antoine 27–28; *Te Deum* 28, 48

Chaucer, Geoffrey 9
Chopin, Frédéric 92–94;
    Nocturne in E flat,
    Op. 9 No. 2 100; *Piano*
    Concerto No. 1 101;
    Prelude No. 1 ('Raindrop')
    100; *Waltz in D flat, Op. 64*
    No. 1 ('Minute') 100
Christianity 4, 47
Clarke, Jeremiah 32; *The*
    Prince of Denmark's
    March 32, 49; *Trumpet*
    Voluntary 32
Classical period xiii, 2,
    51–77, 79–80, 81, 103,
    138, 144, 245
Clementi, Muzio 81–82
Coates, Eric, *The Dambusters*
    March 231
Cocteau, Jean 173
Colbran, Isabella 85
Cologne 128
concerto grosso 23, 29
Copland, Aaron xv, 192,
    195, 196, 230;
    Appalachian Spring 195,
    206; *Billy the Kid* 195;
    Fanfare for the Common
    Man 195, 205; *Rodeo*
    195, 206
Corelli, Arcangelo 28–29;
    Concerto Grosso, Op. 6
    No. 8 ('The Christmas
    Concerto') 48

Coventry Cathedral 201
Cromwell, Thomas 12
Crosby, Bing xv
Crown Film Unit 201
Cui, César 106
Czech National Symphony
    Orchestra 242

Dahl, Dr Nikolai 160
Daimler, Gottlieb 80
Daldry, Stephen 215
Darwin, Charles 176
Davies, Peter Maxwell
    210–211, 215, 223;
    Antarctic Symphony 210;
    Farewell to Stromness
    211, 227; *Taverner* 12,
    210
Davis, Carl 218; *The French*
    Lieutenant's Woman 227;
    The World at War 227
de Falla, Manuel 120–121;
    The Three-Cornered Hat
    121
Debussy, Claude 121,
    170–172, 174; *Clair de*
    Lune (Suite bergamasque)
    203; *La mer* 203; *Prélude*
    à l'après-midi d'un faune
    203
Decca Records 224
Delibes, Léo 129; *Coppélia*
    129, 131; *Lakmé* 129,
    131; *Sylvia* 129, 131

Delius, Frederick 178–179, 181, 222; *Appalachia* 178; *Brigg Fair: An English Rhapsody* 179; *La Calinda* 204; *On Hearing the First Cuckoo in Spring* 204; *The Walk in the Paradise Garden* 204

Diaghilev, Sergei 121, 173, 186, 188; Ballets Russes 174, 186

Diana, Princess of Wales 214

Disney, Walt 107, 229

Dittersdorf, Karl Ditters von 60; *Harp Concerto* 75

Divine Comedy, The 221

Dover Priory 13

Doyle, Patrick, *Sense and Sensibility* 231

Dresden 84

Dublin 44, 81, 125; Trinity College 125

Dufay, Guillaume 10–11; *L'Homme armé* 11

Dukas, Paul 121, 229

Dunstable, John 10–11; *Preco preheminencie* 18

Durazzo, Count Giacomo 34

Durey, Louis 191

Dvořák, Antonín 113–114, 184; *Cello Concerto* 115;
Rusalka 115; *Serenade for Strings* 115; *Slavonic Dances* 115; *Symphony No. 9 ('From the New World')* 114, 115

EA Games xvi, 242

Early Music 1–19, 22, 48, 210; Movement 2

Ecclesium 226

Edward VI 12

Einaudi, Ludovico 219–220; *I Giorni* 228; *Le Onde* 228

Eisenstein, Sergei 189

Elgar, Edward 31, 117, 125, 149–152, 154, 175, 179, 197, 210; *Cello Concerto* 151, 165; *Chanson de matin* 165; *Enigma Variations* 150–151, 165; *Pomp and Circumstance March No. 1* 151, 165; *Salut d'amour* 165; *Serenade for Strings* 165; *The Black Knight* 150; *The Light of Life* 150; *Violin Concerto* 180

Elizabeth I 3–4, 12, 14

EMI Classics 33

England 3, 4, 11, 14, 25, 31, 43, 58, 98, 113, 120, 122, 123, 175, 179, 201, 210, 231; Bank of

151–152; Church of 12, 26

Eric Whitacre Singers 225

Esterházy, Prince Paul 58

Fantasia 107, 229

Fauré, Gabriel 148–149; *Cantique de Jean Racine* 165; *Dolly Suite* 165; *Pelléas et Mélisande* 165; *Requiem* 149, 165

Fenby, Eric 179

Field, John 81–82; *Piano Concerto No. 2* 99

'Fight for the Right' 124

Finland 116

Finzi, Gerald 179; *Eclogue* 204

First World War 121, 127, 175, 176, 190

Françaix, Jean 192; *Malabar Jasmine (L'horloge de flore)* 192, 205

France 4, 27, 46, 53, 61, 123, 128, 129, 130, 138, 149, 152, 173, 175, 186

Franck, César 131, 148; *Panis Angelicus* 132

Franco of Cologne 8

Franco-Prussian War 129

Frederick the Great 56

Gagarin, Yuri 199

George I 43–44

George II 44, 54

George III 54

George V 125

Germany 1, 37, 38, 43, 45, 74, 83, 123, 125, 152, 156, 157, 190, 219

Gershwin, George 194–195, 196; *An American in Paris* 194, 206; *Porgy and Bess* 194, 206; *Piano Concerto* 205; *Rhapsody in Blue* 194, 205

Giazotto, Remo 33

Gibbons, Orlando 25–26; *This is the Record of John* 48

Gilbert and Sullivan 123, 128; *HMS Pinafore* 123, 127; *Princess Ida* 123; *The Mikado* 123, 127; *The Pirates of Penzance* 123; *The Yeomen of the Guard* 123; *Trial by Jury* 123

Gilbert, W. S. 123

Girò, Anna 35

Glass, Philip 192, 214–215, 216, 230; *Koyaanisqatsi* 227; *Kundun* 227; *The Hours* 215, 227; *Violin Concerto* 215, 227

Glazunov, Alexander 185; *Saxophone Concerto* 185; *The Seasons* 205

Glennie, Evelyn 223

Glinka, Mikhail 104–105,
112; *A Life for the Tsar*
105; *Kamarinskaya* 111;
Russlan and Ludmilla
105, 111

Gluck, Christoph Willibald
von 54–55, 56, 128, 147;
Orpheus and Euridice 75

Goldsmith, Jerry 231; *Star
Trek* 231; *The Omen* 231

Goodall, Howard 222–223;
Blackadder 222;
Enchanted Voices 222,
228; *Eternal Light:
A Requiem* 222, 228;
Mr Bean 222; *QI* 222;
Red Dwarf 222; *The Lord
is My Shepherd* 228;
The Catherine Tate Show
222; *The Vicar of Dibley*
222

Górecki, Henryk 211–212;
Symphony No. 3 211,
227

Gounod, Charles 98, 147;
'Ave Maria' 98; *Faust* 98;
Mors et Vita 98, 101;

Grainger, Percy 180–181;
*Music for an English
Country Garden* 204

Granados, Enrique 120

Gravesend 108

Greenaway, Peter 216

Gregorian Chant 5

Gregory I, Pope 4–5, 245

Grieg, Edvard 116–117,
181; *Holberg Suite* 118;
Lyric Pieces 116; *Peer
Gynt Suite No. 1* 118;
Piano Concerto 116, 118

Griskey, Mark 242;
Command & Conquer
242; *Harry Potter* 242;
The Lord of the Rings 242

Guido d'Arezzo 6

Hamburg 37, 42, 56, 143

Handel, George Frideric
29, 38, 41–45, 46, 147;
*Arrival of the Queen of
Sheba (Solomon)* 49;
Messiah 44, 49; *Music for
the Royal Fireworks* 44;
'Ombra mai fu'(Xerxes)
49; *Rinaldo* 43; *Water
Music* 44, 49; *'Zadok the
Priest'* 44, 49

Hannigan, James 242;
Command & Conquer
242; *Harry Potter* 242;
The Lord of the Rings
242

Hardy, Thomas 177, 179

Hargreaves, James 52

harmony 22–23

Hawes, Patrick 221–222;
Blue in Blue 221, 228;

Highgrove Suite 221, 228; *Into the Light* 221, 228; '*Quanta qualia*' 221
Haydn, Joseph 52, 55, 56–59, 64, 68, 69–70, 84, 144; *Cello Concertos Nos. 1* and *2* 75; *London Symphonies* 59; *Symphony No. 1* ('*The Clock*') 59, 75; *Symphony No. 45* ('*Farewell*') 58; *The Seasons* 75
Haydn, Michael 84
Henry VIII 12
Herrmann, Bernard, *Psycho* 231
Hess, Nigel, *Ladies in Lavender* 231, 237
Hildegard of Bingen 7–8, 15; '*A Feather on the Breath of God*' 18
Hitchcock, Alfred 221
Holland 69, 123
Hollywood 186; Bowl 180
Holst, Gustav 124, 175, 176–177; '*I Vow to Thee My Country*' 177; *St Paul's Suite* 204; *The Planets* 177, 204
Honegger, Arthur 191
Horner, James xvi, 235–236; *Star Trek II: The Wrath of Khan* 236; *Titanic* 236, 237

Howard, Ron 236

'Impressionist' composers 171, 173
Isserlis, Steven 214
Italy 11, 14, 16, 36, 61, 64, 84, 85, 105, 138, 139, 152, 190, 210, 219

Jackson, Peter 235
James II 31
Janáček, Leoš 114–115; *Glagolitic Mass* 115; *Jenůfa* 115; *Sinfonietta* 115; *The Cunning Little Vixen* 115
Japan 241
Jenkins, Karl 217–218; *Adiemus: Songs of Sanctuary* 217, 227; *Palladio* 227; *Requiem* 218; *The Armed Man: A Mass for Peace* 11, 217, 227
'Jesuit Reductions' 47
Joffé, Roland 47
John of Fonsete, '*Sumer is icumen in*' 8
Julius III, Pope 15

Kennedy, Nigel 33
Khachaturian, Aram 190–191, 230; *Gayaneh* 191; *Piano Concerto* 190;

Khachaturian, Aram (CONTD.)
Spartacus 191, 205;
Violin Concerto 190
Kirkhope, Grant 239; Banjo
Kazoote 243; Kingdoms of
Amalur 243; Viva Piñata
243
Kodály, Zoltán 183–184;
Háry János Suite 205
Korngold, Eric 230
Kreisler, Fritz 179–180;
Schön Rosmarin 204

Lancaster, House of 3
Lavigra, Vincenzo 139
Layton, Stephen 224
Le Mans, Conservatoire 192
Leeds 198; Festival 113
Lehár, Franz 184–185;
Gold and Silver Waltz
205; The Merry Widow
184–185
Leipzig 37, 40, 95, 116,
178; Gewandhaus
concert hall 242;
Gewandhaus Orchestra
92; University 37, 158
Lenin, Vladimir 188
Leningrad, siege of 199
Lennertz, Christopher 242;
Command & Conquer
242; Harry Potter 242;
The Lord of the Rings
242

Leoncavallo, Ruggero
154–155; La bohème
155; Pagliacci 155, 166
Lieder see Schubert, Franz
Lincoln Cathedral 13
Liszt, Franz 96–98, 147,
152, 182, 185; Hungarian
Rhapsody No. 2 101;
Liebestraum No. 3 101;
Piano Concerto No. 2
101; Rhapsodie espagnole
101
Litolff, Henry 138; Scherzo
(Concerto sinfonique
No. 4) 138, 163
Liverpool 120; Cathedral
219
London 14, 43, 59, 63, 81,
123, 151, 155; Alhambra
Theatre 121; City
124; Guildhall School
of Music and Drama
126, 221; Highgate
School 213; Houses of
Parliament 22; Hyde
Park 44; King's College
216; Lloyds of 124;
Philharmonic Orchestra
218, 235, 241; Royal
Academy of Music
213, 216, 217; Royal
Albert Hall 125; Royal
College of Music 125,
126, 175; Royal Opera

House, Covent Garden
57, 84; Savoy Theatre
123; Sinfonietta 211;
St Paul's Cathedral 32,
54; St Paul's School for
Girls 177; Symphony
Orchestra 241, 253;
Westminster Abbey 31,
32, 45, 125, 214, 225, 226
Los Angeles 162, 232–233;
Walt Disney Concert
Hall 242
Louis XIV 26, 27
Louis XV 46
Lucas, George 233
Lucerne, Lake 71, 161
Lully, Jean-Baptiste 26–27,
46; *Alceste* 48

MacCunn, Hamish 126;
*The Land of the Mountain
and the Flood* 126, 127
MacDowell, Edward 152;
Piano Concerto 152;
To a Wild Rose 165
Machaut, Guillaume de
8–9; *Messe de Notre
Dame* 9, 18
Macmillan, James 223; *Veni
Emanuel* 223
madrigals 14
Mahler, Gustav 117,
155–156; *Symphony
No. 1 ('Titan')* 166;

*Symphony No. 3
('Resurrection')* 166;
Symphony No. 5 166;
*Symphony No. 8
('Symphony of a
Thousand')* 156, 166
Malfatti, Therese 73
Malmö Symphonic
Orchestra 242
Malone, Gareth 225
Malvern Hills 150
Manchester 53; Royal
Manchester College
210; 'School' 210
Marcellus, Pope 15
Marconi, Guglielmo 80
Marianelli, Dario 232;
Atonement 232
Marine Band 193
Mary I 12
Mary, Queen 31
Mascagni, Pietro 153–154;
Cavalleria Rusticana 154,
155, 166
Massenet, Jules 129–130;
Le Cid 130; *Manon* 130;
Thaïs 130, 131
Matthews, Colin, 'Pluto' 177
McCartney, Paul 218–219;
Liverpool Oratorio
218–219, 227; *Ocean's
Kingdom* 219; *Standing
Stone* 219, 228; *Working
Classical* 219

Mealor, Paul 225–226;
A Tender Light 226; 'Ave
Verum' 226; Coventry
Carol 226; The Call
to Wisdom 226; 'Ubi
Caritas' 225, 227;
'Wherever You Are' 225
Meck, Nadezhda von 111
Medieval period 2, 18, 245
Mendelssohn, Fanny 92
Mendelssohn, Felix 90–92;
A Midsummer Night's
Dream 91, 100; Elijah
92; Hebrides Overture
92, 100; Octet 91; 'O for
the wings of a dove' 100;
'Scottish' Symphony 92;
Songs Without Words
100; Symphony No. 4
('Italian') 100
'Mighty Handful, The'
106–107
Milan 47, 54, 139, 219;
Conservatoire 139, 153
Milhaud, Darius 191
Military Wives 225
minimalism 214–215, 216
Monteverdi, Claudio 17, 54,
128; La Favola d'Orfeo
17, 54–55; Vespers for the
Blessed Virgin 17, 19
Montgolfier, Joseph and
Jacques 53
Morricone, Ennio 230;

The Good, The Bad
and the Ugly 230; The
Mission 47, 230, 237
Moscheles, Ignaz 92
Moscow 158, 159, 162;
Bolshoi 188–189;
Conservatoire 158;
Gnessin Music Academy
190
Mozart, Leopold 62–63, 64;
Toy Symphony 75
Mozart, Nannerl 63
Mozart, Wolfgang Amadeus
25, 38, 52, 55, 56,
62–70, 69, 70, 71,
72, 73, 81, 144, 147,
243, 246; 'Ave verum
corpus' 226; Clarinet
Concerto xv, 76, 229;
Così fan tutte 64, 76;
Don Giovanni 64, 76;
Horn Concerto No. 4 76;
'Laudate Dominum' 75;
Piano Concerto No. 21
76; Requiem 66, 75, 224;
Serenade No. 13 ('Eine
kleine Nachtmusik') 76,
229; Symphony No. 41
('Jupiter') 76; The Magic
Flute 64, 67, 76; The
Marriage of Figaro 64, 76
Munich 63, 84, 158, 190
Music Academy of Bologna
85

Mussolini, Benito 190
Mussorgsky, Modest
    106–108, 229; *A Night
    on the Bare Mountain*
    107, 111; *Boris Godunov*
    107, 111; *Pictures at an
    Exhibition* 107, 111
Myers, Stanley 236–237;
    Gladiator 237; *Pirates of
    the Caribbean* 237

Naples, Conservatoire 154
National Children's
    Orchestras of Great
    Britain 253
National Youth Orchestra of
    Great Britain 253
New York 113, 123, 152,
    162, 186, 195, 218, 219,
    220, 232; Greenwich
    Village 220; Juilliard
    School 214, 224,
    232; Manhattan 233;
    Philharmonic Orchestra
    202; State University 220
New Zealand Symphony
    Orchestra 235
Newbury String Players 179
Newton, Isaac 22
Nijinsky, Vaslav 186
Norway 116
Novák, Vítězslav 114
Nyman, Michael 216; *The
    Cook, The Thief, His Wife

    and Her Lover* 216; *The
    Draughtsman's Contract*
    216; *The Piano* 217, 227,
    237

Offenbach, Jacques
    128–129, 135, *Orpheus
    in the Underworld*
    128, 131; *The Tales of
    Hoffmann* 129, 131
Olivier, Laurence 198
opera 16, 46, 54–55, 84, 85,
    140–141, 152–153
Orchestra of Opera North 253
Orkney 211
Orthodox Church 213

Pachelbel, Johann, *Canon
    in D* 30, 48
Padua: Cappella del Santo
    36; University 36
Paganini, Niccolò 82–83,
    88, 96; *Violin Concerto
    No. 2* 99
Palestrina, Giovanni Pierluigi
    da 15–16; *Missa Papae
    Marcelli* 15, 19
Paraguay 47
Paris 46, 63, 85, 87, 89, 93,
    98, 120, 121, 122, 131,
    155, 171, 172, 175, 178,
    195, 214; Conservatoire
    129, 130, 131, 147, 149,
    152, 172, 174, 179, 192;

Paris (CONTD.) La Madeleine 147, 148; Montmartre 171, 172; Montparnasse Cemetery 148; St Sulpice 130; Théâtre Lyrique 129

Parry, Hubert 124–125, 126; 'Blest Pair of Sirens' 124; 'I Was Glad' 124, 127; Jerusalem 124, 127

Pärt, Arvo 212–213; Spiegel im Spiegel 227

Pasta, Giuditta 87

Paul V, Pope 17

Pears, Peter 201

Peri, Jacopo 16–17, 128; Dafne 16–17; Euridice 17, 19

Perkins, Captain J. R. 220

Philadelphia Orchestra 229

Philharmonia Orchestra 241, 242, 253

Philip Glass Ensemble 215

plainchant 5, 8, 15, 18, 245

Pollack, Sydney 234

polyphony 8–9, 15, 18

Polyphony (choir) 224

Ponchielli, Amilcare 229

Portman, Rachel, Chocolat 231

Poulenc, Francis Jean Marcel 191–192; Gloria 191; Les biches 191, 205;

Organ Concerto 205; The Story of Babar, the Little Elephant 192, 205

Prague 36, 84, 93, 113, 114, 115; Conservatoire 184; Opera 115

Prokofiev, Sergei xv, 87–189, 191, 230; Alexander Nevsky 189; Ivan the Terrible 189; Lieutenant Kijé 205; Peter and the Wolf 205; Romeo and Juliet 188, 205; Symphony No. 1 ('Classical') 205; Symphony No. 5 188; The Love for Three Oranges 187, 205; Violin Concerto No. 2 188; War and Peace 189

Protestants/Protestantism 12, 14

Puccini, Giacomo 152–153; Gianni Schicchi 166; La bohème 153, 155, 166; Madam Butterfly 153, 166; Manon Lescaut 153; Tosca 153, 166; Turandot 153, 166

Purcell, Henry 25, 31, 54, 125, 128; Abdelazar 48, 201; 'Come Ye Sons of Art' 48; King Arthur 31; Trumpet Tune and Air

in D 48; 'When I Am
Laid in Earth' (*Dido and
Aeneas*) 31–32, 48
Pushkin, Alexander 61

Rachmaninov, Sergei
159–162; *Aleko* 159;
Piano Concerto No. 1
159; *Piano Concerto
No. 2* 160–161, 167,
229; *Piano Concerto
No. 3* 167; *Rhapsody on
a Theme of Paganini* 167;
Symphony No. 1 160;
Symphony No. 2 167;
Vocalise 167
Raff, Joachim 152
Rameau, Jean-Philippe 46;
Les Indes galantes 50
Randolph, David 142
Ravel, Maurice 107, 121,
173–175, 192; *Boléro*
173, 174, 203; *Daphnis et
Chloé* 174, 204; *L'heure
espagnole, Valses nobles
et sentimentales* 174;
Le tombeau de Couperin
175, 204; *Pavane pour
une infante défunte* 203;
*Piano Concerto in D for
the left hand* 204
Reger, Max 157–158; *Cello
Suite No. 1* 167
Reich, Steve 214, 216

Renaissance period 2,
10–19, 222, 245
Respighi, Ottorino 189–190;
Fountains of Rome 189;
Pines of Rome 189, 205;
The Birds 189
Revolution (1848) 130
Riche de la Poupelinière,
Alexandre le 46
Rieu, André 133–134
Riley, Terry 214
Rimsky-Korsakov, Nikolai
106–109, 185, 189;
Capriccio espagnol 112;
Flight of the Bumblebee
112; *Scheherazade* 109,
111; *Symphony No. 1*
108
Rodrigo, Joaquín 196–197;
Concierto de Aranjuez
197, 206; *Fantasia para
un gentilhombre* 206
Roerich, Nicholas 186
Romantic period 51, 68, 74,
80, 81, 83, 84, 96, 140,
156, 159, 163, 181, 194,
196, 222, 230, 245; Early
Romantics 79–101;
Late Romantics 81, 96;
Nationalist Romantics
81, 103–138
Rome 11, 12, 15, 31, 35,
47, 154; Academy of
St Cecilia 189;

Rome (CONTD.) Accademia di
Belle Arti 190
Roosevelt, Franklin D. 130
Rossini, Gioachino 84–86,
87, 97, 147; 'Stabat
Mater' 86, 100; The
Barber of Seville 85, 99;
The Thieving Magpie 100;
William Tell 85, 100
Royal Liverpool
Philharmonic Orchestra
146, 253
Royal Northern Sinfonia
Orchestra 253
Royal Philharmonic Society
113
Royal Scottish National
Orchestra 146, 241,
253
Royal Shakespeare Company
218
Rozario, Patricia 214
Russia 74, 123, 159, 161,
162, 170, 185, 186, 187,
188, 189, 195
Russian Revolution 161
Rutter, John 215–216; A
Gaelic Blessing 227; For
the Beauty of the Earth
227; Requiem 215, 227

Saint-Saëns, Camille
146–148; Carnival of
the Animals 147–148,
165; Danse Macabre
165; L'Assassinat du
duc de Guise xv, 229;
Samson and Delilah 147;
Symphony No. 3 ('Organ')
148, 165; Violin Sonata
No. 1 165
Salieri, Antonio 61, 66;
Flute and Oboe Concerto
75
Salzburg 62; Mozarteum
190; Prince Archbishop
of 63, 65
Sand, George 94
Satie, Erik 172–173, 180;
Five Grins or Mona
Lisa's Moustache 172;
Gnossiennes 203;
Gymnopédies 173, 203;
Menus for Childish
Purposes 172; Parade
173; Sketches and
Exasperations of a Big
Boob Made of Wood 172;
Things Seen from the
Right and Left without
Spectacles 172; Three
Pear-Shaped Pieces 172;
Veritable Flabby Preludes
(for a Dog) 172; Vexations
172–173; Waltz of the
Chocolate Almonds 172
Saxe-Weimar Duke of
39–40

Saxe-Weissenfels, Duke
of 42
Scandinavia 116, 161
Scarlatti, Alessandro 45
Scarlatti, Domenico 45–46;
Sonata in A 50
Schaffer, Peter 61
Schoenberg, Arnold
181–182, 194, 196, 199;
Verklärte Nacht 205
Schola Cantorum 5
Schubert, Franz 73, 87–88,
97, 229; *'Ave Maria'*
100; *Der Erlkönig* 87;
'Gretchen am Spinnrade'
87; *Marche Militaire No. 1*
100; *Piano Quintet in A*
('Trout') 100; *Rosamunde*
1900; *Symphony No. 5*
100; *Symphony No. 8*
('Unfinished Symphony')
88
Schumann, Clara 94–96,
143, 145
Schumann, Robert 92,
94–96, 143; *Fantasy in C*
101; *Kinderszenen* 101;
Piano Concerto 101;
Träumerei 101
Scotland 3, 91, 116, 231
Scriabin, Alexander
158–159; *Etude in D*
sharp minor, Op. 8 No. 12
167; *Poem of Fire* 159

Second World War 156,
183, 196, 211
Shimomura, Yoko, *Kingdom*
Hearts 243
Shore, Howard xvi, 235;
Hobbit trilogy 235; *Lord*
of the Rings 235, 237
Short, Nigel 226
Shostakovich, Dmitri xv,
198–199, 230; *Jazz*
Suites Nos 1 and 2 199,
206; *Lady Macbeth*
of the Mtensk District
199; *Piano Concerto*
No. 2 206; *'Romance'*
(The Gadfly) 198, 206;
Symphony No. 1 198;
Symphony No. 5 199,
206; *Symphony No. 7*
199; *The Assault on*
Beautiful Gorky 198,
206; *The Nose* 198
Sibelius, Jean 116–118;
En Saga 117; *Finlandia*
117, 119; *Karelia Suite*
118; *Kullervo* 117;
Symphony No. 5 118,
119; *The Swan of Tuonela*
118; *Valse Triste* 119;
Violin Concerto 118, 119
Sitwell, Edith 198
'Six, Les' 191
Skeet, Andrew 241
Slovenia 36

Smetana, Bedřich 112–113;
    Má Vlast 113, 115; *The
    Bartered Bride* 115
Smithson, Harriet 89
Soft Machine 217
Somme, Battle of the 127
sonata 23, 56
Soule, Jeremy 239; *The
    Elder Scrolls* 239, 243
Sousa, John Philip 193;
    'Stars and Stripes Forever'
    193; *The Washington
    Post* 205
South America 46
Spain 1, 61, 119, 121, 123
Spanish Civil War 121
Spielberg, Steven 233, 236
Spohr, Louis 74; *Clarinet
    Concerto No. 1* 77
St Petersburg 82, 159, 185;
    Conservatoire 187, 198
Stadler, Anton xv
Stalin, Joseph 189, 198, 199
Stanford, Sir Charles Villiers
    125; *Magnificat in G* 127
Stanley, John 179
Starr, Ringo 213
Steiner, Max 231; *Gone with
    the Wind* 231, 237
Stokowski, Leopold 122,
    229
Stone, Oliver 196, 236
Stopford, Philip, 'Ave Verum'
    228

Strauss family 133–134,
    156
Strauss Jnr, Johann
    132–134; *By the Beautiful
    Blue Danube* 133, 135;
    Die Fledermaus 133,
    135; *Pizzicato Polka* 134
Strauss Snr, Johann 132,
    135; *Radetzky March*
    132, 135; *Tales from
    the Vienna Woods*
    135; *Thunder and
    Lightning Polka* 135;
    Tritsch-Tratsch Polka 135
Strauss, Eduard 133
Strauss, Josef 133, 134;
    Pizzicato Polka 134
Strauss, Richard 156–157;
    Also Sprach Zarathustra
    157, 166, 229; *Ariadne
    auf Naxos* 157; *Der
    Rosenkavalier* 157; *Four
    Last Songs* 157, 166;
    Salome 157
Stravinsky, Igor 108–109,
    121, 160, 174, 185–188,
    196, 213, 229; *Petrushka*
    186; *The Firebird* 186,
    205; *The Rite of Spring*
    205
string quartet 56
Strom, Ella Viola 180
Stuttgart 84, 93
Suk, Josef 114

Sullivan, Arthur 122–124;
    Ivanhoe 124, 127;
    'Onward! Christian
    Soldiers' 124; *Symphony
    in E* 124, 127; *see also*
    Gilbert and Sullivan
Suppé, Franz von 134–135;
    Light Cavalry 135;
    *Morning, Noon and Night
    in Vienna* 135; *Poet and
    Peasant* 135
Süssmayr, Franz Xaver 67
Sweden 242
Switzerland 158, 161, 186,
    190
symphony 56

Tailleferre, Germaine 191
Talbot, Joby 220–221; *Once
    Around the Sun* 220,
    228; Talbot, *Robbie
    the Reindeer* 221; *The
    Hitchhiker's Guide to the
    Galaxy* 221; *The League
    of Gentlemen* 221; *The
    Lodger* 221
Tallis, Thomas 12–13, 14,
    25; *Lamentations* 13;
    Mass for Four Voices 13;
    'Spem in alium' 13, 18
Tartini, Giuseppe 36–37;
    *Sonata in G minor for
    solo violin: 'The Devil's
    Trill'* 49

Tavener, John 212–214,
    223; *Song for Athene*
    214, 227; *The Lamb* 227;
    The Protecting Veil 214,
    227; *The Whale* 213
Taverner, John 12, 210;
    *Mass: 'The Western
    Wynde'* 18
Taylor, John 41
Tchaikovsky, Pyotr Ilyich
    109–111, 160, 229;
    1812 Overture 112;
    Eugene Onegin 110;
    Piano Concerto No. 1
    110, 112; *Romeo and
    Juliet* 112; *Swan Lake*
    110, 112; *Symphony
    No. 6 ('Pathétique')* 112;
    Nutcracker 110, 112;
    The Sleeping Beauty 110,
    112; *Violin Concerto*
    110, 112
Telemann, Georg Philipp
    37–38, 41, 56; *Concerto
    in D for trumpet and
    strings* 49
Tenebrae 226
Thames: Estuary 108; River
    44
Todd, Will, 'Lux et Veritas'
    228
Toscanini, Arturo 153
Trevisana, Paolina 36
troubadours 9

Turnage, Mark-Anthony
223–224
twenty-first century
209–243

Uematsu, Nobuo 239; *Final
Fantasy* 239, 243
UK 134, 193, 218, 241,
242
Ungar, Jay 220; *The Ashokan
Farewell* 220, 228
Upshaw, Dawn 211
USA 3, 53, 113, 114, 120,
146, 156, 161, 162, 170,
235, 243; *see also* South
America

Vatican 24, 64

Vaughan-Williams, Ralph
xv, 124, 127, 175–176,
179, 222, 230; *English
Folksong Suite* 204;
*Fantasia on a Theme of
Thomas Tallis* 176, 204;
Fantasia on Greensleeves
204; *On Wenlock Edge*
175; *Symphony No. 2
('London')* 127, 176, 204;
Symphony No. 5 204;
The Lark Ascending 176,
204; *The Wasps* 175
Venice 142, 190; La Pietà
orphans institute 35–36;

St Stephen's Cathedral
57
Verdi, Giuseppe 138–140,
152; *Aida* 139, 153,
163; *Il trovatore* 164;
La forza del destino 163;
La traviata 164; *Nabucco*
164; *Requiem* 140, 164;
Rigoletto 163
verismo 154
Victoria, Queen 80, 92
video games xvi, 238–243
Vienna 36, 55, 63, 67, 69,
70, 84, 85, 88, 93, 123,
133, 134; Conservatoire
156, 179; Sperl Ballroom
132; State Opera 156
Villa-Lobos, Heitor
120–121; *Bachianas
brasileiras* 122; *Chôros*
121
Virginia Tech University:
Minecraft 243;
OperaCraft 243
Vivaldi, Antonio 33–36;
Four Seasons 49; '*Gloria*'
49; '*Nulla in mundo pax
sincera*' 49

Wagner, Richard 96,
140–142, 155; *Das
Rheingold* 141; *Die
Walküre* 141, 164;
Götterdämmerung 141,

164; *Lohengrin* 164, 219; *Parsifal* 142; *Siegfried* 141; *Tannhäuser* 164; *The Flying Dutchman* 164; *Tristan and Isolde* 164

Waltham Abbey 13

Walton, William xv, 197–198, 230; *Belshazzar's Feast* 198, 206; *Crown Imperial* 198, 206; *Façade* 206; *Orb and Sceptre* 198, 206; *Spitfire Prelude and Fugue* 206; *Viola Concerto* 198, 206

Warbeck, Stephen, *Shakespeare in Love* 231

Ward, Thomas F. 178

Warner Classics 33

Weber, Aloysia 65

Weber, Carl Maria von 83–84; *Clarinet Concerto No. 1* 99; *Der Freischütz* 84; Oberon 84

Weber, Constanze 65

Weir, Judith 7, 223

Whitacre, Eric 224–225; *Cloudburst* 224; *Light and Gold* 224; 'Lux Aurumque' 224; 'Sleep' 224; *Water Night* 224; *The Seal Lullaby* 228

'White Christmas' xv

Widor, Charles-Marie 130–131; *Toccata (Organ Symphony No. 5)* 132

Wieck, Clara *see* Schumann, Clara

Wieck, Friedrich 95

Wilcken, Anna Magdalena 40

William the Conqueror 3

Williams, John xvi, 232–233; *E.T.* 237; *Jurassic Park* 237; *Saving Private Ryan* 237; *Schindler's List* 237; *Star Wars* 233; *Sugarland Express* 233

Williams, John (guitarist) 197

Winchester College 32

Wintory, Austin, *Journey* 243

Wiseman, Debbie, *Wilde* 231

Wolf-Ferrari, Ermanno 190; *Intermezzo (Susanna's Secret)* 205

Woolf, Virginia 220

Zimmer, Hans xvi, 236

Zipoli, Domenico 46–47; *Elevazione* 47, 50

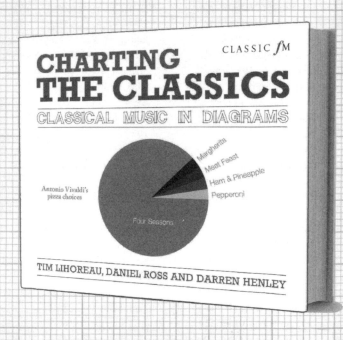

In the same series

The Classic FM Handy Guide to The Orchestra
by Darren Henley

The Classic FM Handy Guide to Classical Recordings by Sam Jackson

The Classic FM Handy Guide to Ballet
by Tim Lihoreau

The Classic FM Handy Guide to Video Game Music
by Daniel Ross

The Classic FM Handy Guide to Film Music
by Rob Weinberg

The Classic FM Handy Guide to Opera
by Rob Weinberg